There are only two kinds of videos,
those that earn you income...
and those that don't

Review Request

If you would recommend this book to others,
please consider writing a 5 star review on <u>Amazon.com</u>.

Make Money on **Amazon** Video Direct

Make Money on

Amazon

Video Direct

The Best Ideas for Your Online Video Marketing Strategy

TRACY FOOTE

TracyTrends

New York, USA

KidsandMoneyToday.com

Visit our website for links to social networks:

Printed in the United States of America
Copyright © 2016 by Tracy Foote
Published by TracyTrends
http://www.TracyTrends.com
Please send all inquiries to:
TracyTrends
c/o T. Foote
27 West 86 Street, Suite 17B
New York, NY 10024
tracytrends@aol.com

Business & Economics / E-Commerce / Internet Marketing
Business & Money / Processes & Infrastructure / E-Commerce
Print Version ISBN 10: 0-9814737-7-6
Print Version ISBN 13: 978-0-9814737-7-2
Library of Congress Control Number: 2016909062
Connect on social networks or comment on our blog at:
https://www.KidsandMoneyToday.com

Contents

FREE Membership for Readers

Receive:
- Amazon Video Direct news
- Video marketing strategies

View the link below to join:

https://www.KidsAndMoneyToday.com/avd/

Preface

When Amazon Video Direct (AVD) began in early 2016, its income opportunities and FREE marketing options intrigued me. Press articles flooded the Internet, saying AVD would be the next competitor to YouTube. Some denied this and wrote about how it would challenge Netflix's live streaming movies. Others claimed the entire program was solely designed to capture more customers to sign up for Amazon Prime, the annual membership program offering both free shipping and free video streaming.

The new Video Direct program allows creators to upload their videos for free to the Amazon platform and earn royalties based on views, rentals, purchases, ads, and a bonus program.

My Amazon experience is founded in books. I've published using Advantage, Createspace, and Kindle. I've already written a book on the power of video marketing using YouTube, but now, I think AVD might be a better fit for my business needs. I suspect the same will be true for many other marketers, and I share my ideas throughout this book.

YouTube can act as a pathway to bring customers over to the Amazon platform, but one challenge is that people go to YouTube for research and entertainment. Most viewers do not have buying on their minds, so marketers have to hope they notice and click on a purchasing link. In sharp contrast, the Amazon customer arrives on site with the main goal of making a purchase.

Google owns YouTube, and this makes it extremely easy to rank YouTube videos in Google search results. These YouTube videos can then include links that entice viewers to click over to Amazon. Fortunately, Amazon pages are also fairly easy to rank in Google, and now, the customer will be on the right platform for a sales conversion!

It seems Amazon Video Direct solves two immediate marketing problems: the customer location and mindset.

AVD is certainly not just a benefit for authors. Anyone with a physical product can establish their item in an Amazon listing using the *Seller Central Program*. After creating a listing, you can collect orders and ship them yourself (which is called Merchant Fulfilled), or you can use Amazon's warehouse program (which is called Fulfilled by Amazon (FBA)) to have Amazon package and ship your items. You can then follow the same marketing concept of creating videos that highlight your products. The goal is the same. You want viewers to watch your video and then search for and purchase your product on Amazon.

It's not all about physical products. Independent filmmakers, often on a low budget, might turn to Amazon Video Direct as an affordable way to promote or offer their film to the public. There's also room for the hobbyists and social leaders, and instructors are sure to come over from Udemy.com (a site that offers video courses).

Similar to YouTube, anyone can make a video about what they know: gardening, auto repair, cooking, fitness, or any other topic. When this video is watched, Amazon offers several royalty choices for the creator to earn some cash.

The goal of this book is to help rank your videos high so they can be found easily in both Amazon and Google search results. This will increase your exposure, and help you convert this traffic into a source of income. You can make good videos with fancy, high-tech equipment, but they can also be made with smart phones. Because of this, camera and lighting tips are skipped. The focus of this book is on the optimization and monetization of your video marketing process.

At the end of this book, you'll find checklists and a Resource section with helpful links on topics such as: audio, animation, graphics, monetization, and organization.

Amazon Video Direct will change as it continues to develop. It's possible some screenshots that I've included will become outdated. However, usually the general concept stays the same; the button is just moved to a new location to make the page more user friendly. If a layout does change, try an Internet search for the topic, along with words like: tutorial, set-up, help, or the current year. This should bring up the most relevant, up-to-date screenshots to complete any task I've suggested.

In such a case, when you find a step unclear, the best way to contact me is to join my mailing list at:

https://www.kidsandmoneytoday.com/avd/

Once you have joined the list, simply hit reply to any e-mail and you can send me a comment or question.

Tracy Foote
https://www.amazon.com/author/tracyfoote

What is Amazon Video Direct?

The Amazon Video Direct program began in early 2016, allowing users to upload their videos to the Amazon platform. It's possible that Amazon wants to compete with YouTube, Netflix, and Udemy. YouTube allows everything from funny cell phone clips to advanced tutorials. Netflix is well known for streaming movies, and Udemy is a platform that caters toward instructors offering video courses. Surprisingly, many people have still not heard of Udemy. On the contrary, it seems a challenge to find someone who has not heard of Amazon.com, so when comparing these platforms, Amazon certainly brings some excitement to the table!

Venues like YouTube, Vimeo, Netflix, iTunes, HULU, and Udemy are often on a filmmaker's watch list. Even Facebook has videos now. These all have an extended audience, and some have features that Amazon Video Direct is missing. For example, some allow outbound links right on their platform, which helps create inbound links to your own website. There are definitely pros of using these other platforms, so if you are already there, don't stop using them.

Filmmakers and producers are often on a tight budget, and this budget runs even tighter after production, when it comes time for release and marketing. Sometimes the goal changes to "make the film available to the world" instead of "take home a profit." That's where free online distribution, with no application approval process can help.

Pros of Amazon's Online Distribution

In many ways, it seems like Amazon's goal has always been to capture a valid e-mail and physical address for everyone, worldwide, and what marketer wouldn't like to have access, even if somewhat limited, to reaching the customers on this list?

List building is touted as the backbone of business growth. You can build one with your own website. You can grow a list using social media platforms like Facebook, Pinterest, and Twitter. However, this takes a lot of time. It's much faster and less effort to connect with someone who already has a *List* and create either a one time or long term joint venture partnership. Uploading videos to Amazon Video Direct is just another joint venture. Income will be created and split between both parties involved.

Amazon is a powerful partner for businesses to connect to. It has authority in Google's eyes. It's a well established website that has value to visitors. If you begin your own website or establish a presence on a social media platform, it will take some time for Google to rank these pages. You will find it much easier to rank your Amazon video URL.

Features

Some features that make Amazon Video Direct attractive are:

1. *Update Videos:* If you need to make any changes, you can re-upload a video and the URL containing that video does not change. Videos on topics like accounting, where you might update a tax table, can be updated each year and the page will retain all the history of views and reviews.

2. *No Entry or Operational Fee:* You can upload your videos for free and there is no monthly or annual charge to keep them running.

3. *No Account Approval Process:* While each video will be reviewed for compliance with Amazon's Terms of Service (TOS), anyone can create an account and begin uploading videos immediately.

4. *Access to a Buying Audience:* Visitors to Amazon expect to pay money. They are not surprised by "Buy Now" offers.

5. *Extensive Choice of Playback on Multiple Devices:* Amazon Prime Customers can stream unlimited movies and episodes on a TV, laptop, Fire TV, smart phone or other device.

6. *Income Opportunities:* You can participate in revenue share for ad impressions, rentals, purchases, monthly subscriptions, or any combination of these.

7. *No Skipping Ads:* When you turn ads on, there is no option for the user to skip an ad (as found on YouTube) so you are guaranteed to be paid some revenue.

Goals

Business owners usually have multiple objectives when choosing Amazon Video Direct. Some common goals are:

1. *Earn income from Amazon*:

   — *Ads:* Amazon runs these before your video plays. You could create tons of video content that people want to watch and collect royalties from pre-roll ads.

   — *Views:* You can also earn royalties based on the hours watched by Amazon Prime customers.

   — *Fees:* You can charge a rental, purchase, or subscription fee for your videos. Most likely these videos will be from creators like course instructors and independent filmmakers.

   — *Monthly Bonus Share*: Top video creators share in the *Star* a bonus program.

2. *Increased Company Sales:* Videos like product reviews and how-to tutorials focus on company sales conversion. The aim is to lead the viewer to a product or service offered either on or off Amazon.

3. *Exposure:* These videos bring exposure to brand names, a product, a cause, or a charity.

4. *Entertainment:* These videos focus on customer enjoyment. These will include topics like a stand-up comic or music bands, but could also include things like funny cat videos or wedding proposals.

5. *Traffic:* The main goal of this type of video is to entice the user to go to another location, usually to a product page on either Amazon or another website, or to a sign up page for the purpose of list building. They could include videos about products and services, or education topics like health, legal issues, pet care, and more.

All of these goals tend to overlap. For example, entertainment videos will also bring exposure, possibly traffic, and can certainly earn income through ads and fees. The general overall goal is to use video to market and grow your business.

Advantages of Video Marketing

When you are looking for ways to grab a customer's attention, video has several advantages over print. With Internet articles, your customers often skim ahead, looking for headers and bullet points to help make a split-second decision to stay or hit the back button. This becomes difficult when you present video. You gain additional time to grab a user's attention. You have a little more control when marketing with video.

Video also appeals to curiosity. Put a play button on a page and most people will click it. Put a big arrow saying, "Don't click here" and people will probably click at a higher rate. Curiosity is just one step along a customer's purchasing path. You can use video to connect with these customers.

Article text can be scraped (extracted) by software; stolen and re-purposed (reprinted, rephrased, or plagiarized) onto another website. You might consider converting some text to video to prevent this. Video is more difficult to steal or copy.

Video can also help protect photography and artwork. Internet images are constantly misused or stolen. Copyright violations are difficult to prevent. Four images that you would have displayed on a page could be turned into a simple slide show to help protect them. It's more difficult to extract an image from a video. It requires more time. Instead of simply right clicking a computer mouse and choosing save or copy, the user must pause the video and capture a screen shot. Video can help deter, but not totally prevent, people from stealing your work.

Some things are easier explained when using video. It can portray a message faster. A step-by-step tutorial article could become an instructional video. The visual explanation can create a more understandable sequence. Would you prefer an article on how to change the oil on your car or a video?

Video content is fun to share. Videos are entertainment. They are usually short. Because they are visual, they are appealing. When a friend shares a video, people want to watch. The emotion felt upon receipt is a positive one and one of anticipation. When someone receives an article link from the same friend, there is a much greater chance it might be bookmarked to read later. Articles feel like interruptions. Visuals work better.

You may find less competition with video. Consider a Google search for the very general topic of "remarriage" and you might see 2,460,000 possibilities under the Web results, but only 1,390,000 (almost half the competition) in Video results. This same idea will apply to searching on the Amazon platform.

Video can boost your credibility or your authority on a subject. Amazon viewers will see any reviews your video receives. They can also click and find other videos done by your company. You can use this visual presence on Amazon to connect with your customers. Perhaps take a screenshot of your Amazon video and post it on a blog or social network.

Human nature lures people to join groups. Watch a theatre entrance with two tellers and everyone's in line for window A, yet window B remains empty. Chances are the next person to arrive will go to the end of line A. The presumption is the majority knows best. The mind assumes window B is closed or the teller is busy. People tend to go with the majority. On Amazon, your reviews give a visual indication of the majority.

Customer comments are powerful. They play a role in conversions. If you can choose a gift behind one of two curtains, and your know, two thousand people liked what was behind curtain number one, which curtain would you choose? You can use this psychology in your video marketing. Try to increase the visual cues, the reviews on your Amazon listings.

Videos can also save time spent with customers. They can be used to screen customers in order to work with a narrow, extremely targeted audience.

You should mimic the strategy of realtors. They put house videos online in order to screen and filter their leads. When their customers call, the realtor knows they have already seen the home. These customers have a higher potential to convert than a customer who may have seen an ad in the local paper.

Video provides additional control, sparks curiosity, prevents theft, offers entertainment, may have less competition, and saves you time by filtering leads to reach a highly targeted audience. Keep all these video benefits in mind as you create a successful video marketing plan.

What Type of Advertising Is Allowed?

Amazon Video Direct is brand new, but sellers have been on Amazon for years. Amazon has well established rules as to what you can and cannot do with an Amazon listing. In general, you don't want to take any action that would interrupt the viewing experience for customers. Find more information in *Help* under *Policies and Agreements > Selling Policies* or at this link:

amazon.com/gp/help/customer/display.html?nodeId=200414320

Links are covered in the AVD *Support > Legal > Content Policy Guidelines* under *"Business Promotion and External Links:"*

> "We will not accept content that implies sponsorship or endorsement by Amazon or otherwise mischaracterizes the relationship with Amazon. We will also not accept content that contains any external links or tracking tags.
>
> Examples include:
>
> — Content that implies a partnership with Amazon.
>
> — Content that contains a link to another webpage or takes the customer out of the Amazon Video application."
>
> videodirect.amazon.com/home/help?topicId=201986500

In the strictest sense, this means you cannot include a URL in your synopsis, even an Amazon URL because that would take the user out of the *Amazon Video application,* to another page on Amazon. Listing references as credits at the end of a video should be acceptable, just as movies run ending credits. You might follow that style to include your website, brand name, and any required designations, such as actors or music used. Stating your profession or background experience as an introduction and to give your video some authority should also be acceptable.

Amazon is known to shut down accounts quickly for violations. Just because you see something done in another video doesn't mean it's acceptable. It's possible it was missed during the approval process. Be very careful about pushing this envelope.

Income Opportunities

The first thing to consider is your Return On Investment (ROI). How much return will you receive for the time you put in creating videos? This answer will help you decide if Amazon Video Direct is a good fit for your business.

The monetary benefits from AVD include:

1. *Cash:* You earn money from users either paying to watch your video, watching through Amazon Prime, and/or from ads displayed to the user prior to watching your video. Plus, there is a chance of a Bonus.

2. *Free Exposure:* This is equivalent to cash because you are saving money that you might have used on advertising. This money can now be re-purposed or withdrawn from the business.

3. *Freelance Work:* Once you are skilled at uploading videos to Amazon's platform, you might offer your uploading skills as a service to other businesses. There will be companies who want to outsource this task. They will look for someone to manage their videos. You can fill that need in a joint venture or freelance work.

Royalties

Royalty options are set under the Availability tab when you upload your videos. Help for royalty options is found at:
Support > Getting Started > Royalty Information
https://videodirect.amazon.com/home/help

There are several types of Royalty options:

 • *Free with ads:* Content Providers can make their video free with ads and receive 55% of net advertising revenue. Ads are selected by Amazon, probably based on words you use in your listing and the Genre category. These ads play prior to your video, like the previews one sees in a movie theatre.

- *Included with Amazon Prime:* Content providers earn $0.15 per hour for U.S. streaming ($0.06 for other locations). There is an annual period cap of 500,000 hours per title.

> "For example, if a title has 2.5 hours of streaming from U.S. customers, the payment would be $0.37. We log and calculate customer streaming to the second."

Anyone can submit a video to Amazon for approval. It could be internet marketers, artists, videographers, or independent filmmakers. Some of these people might feel insulted at receiving only $0.15 per hour, while others may be thrilled.

If you do the math, each title has an earnings limit of $75K (500,000 hours multiplied by $0.15). Lengthy filmmakers might scoff at the idea of earnings being capped at 500,000 hours per year, per title. This may impact your perceived self-worth, but it also impacts your budget. If your intention is to create a profit, don't spend over $75K on actors, props, and equipment.

If you don't use the rental or purchase feature, this hourly rate and annual cap should be of little importance to you.

- *Buy or Rent:* Content Providers can choose either or both of these options. In both choices, you receive 50% of the net revenue.

Here's what Amazon tells customers about buying a video:

> "When you buy a video, your viewing rights don't expire, except as detailed in the Terms of Use. You can Watch Now or Download the video to a compatible device.
>
> If you choose Watch Now, the video will instantly stream to your computer and you may later stream it on another compatible device. If you choose Download, you can download the video to two locations. This enables you to watch the video without an Internet connection. You can also transfer a downloaded video to two portable devices.'

When someone buys your video, they will also have access to any updates to the video. Amazon says:

> "For customers who purchased the content, they'll be able to access the updated video at any time, including if you choose to have the video unpublished."

• *Add-on subscriptions:* If you choose to make your video available only to those with add-on subscriptions, you'll also receive 50% of net monthly revenue. An add-on subscription is something offered to Prime members, where they can choose to add a subscription to something like a show found on Showtime.

• *Bonus Program:* Amazon describes the bonus program as *Amazon Video Direct Star* and states:

> "Amazon will distribute a share of $1,000,000 per month as a bonus to the Top 100 titles included with Prime through Amazon Video Direct. This bonus—based on global customer engagement—is incremental to revenue earned from hours streamed, rentals, purchases, monthly subscriptions, and ad impressions. All of your titles included with Prime are automatically eligible."

Sharing a million dollar profit with other film producers is certainly exciting, and if you get started right away, your chances of being one of these people will be greater.

Under the Support tab of AVD, you can find all the program details. It officially began on 1 June 2016. Part of the requirement for eligibility is to offer your video through Amazon Prime:

> "To be eligible, a title must be published to Amazon Video through Amazon Video Direct and made available in Amazon Prime in at least one country. We don't require that titles are exclusive to Amazon Video or Prime. Titles can also be offered with additional availability options, including buy, rent or ad-supported."

Taxes

For U.S. video creators, you need to remember how royalties are different from a typical paycheck. An employer withholds taxes, but no taxes are withheld when Amazon pays you royalties. Sole Proprietors might set some money aside for self-employment tax, plus state and federal income taxes. Other business models like Corporations and LLCs need to follow applicable rules as well. In all types of businesses, quarterly tax estimates might need to be filed. Check with a tax accountant to make sure your company is in compliance and will have no tax liability surprises.

When you've decided that the exposure, monetary gain, and tax terms are beneficial for your business, it's time to set up your account.

Account Setup

Amazon tends to move items around on it's pages. This book will show some screenshots with an emphasis on the concept behind the task at hand. If needed, you can use Google search to research a topic further. The URL to sign up for your account is located at:
https://videodirect.amazon.com/home/landing

You might sign up for a separate account for each niche brand you own or for any freelance work you might do. In such case, you will need a separate e-mail for each of these account.

Some reasons you might want to set up separate accounts are:

1. Sale of your business, course, or film to another company

2. Separate videos pertaining to niche target audiences into groups

3. Outsourcing

4. Retain other income paths in case an account were to ever be shut down by Amazon

Separate accounts allow you to be prepared for future selling opportunities. If a brand has it's own account and is a separate entity from other brands, the transaction to sell will be simplified. This same concept could be applied to those uploading a course containing a set of videos. Perhaps a course should be contained in its own account, if you intend to sell it in the future.

At the time of sale, you would simply transfer the account by turning over or changing the e-mail address and updating the tax information. One can't be sure if Amazon's back-end coding is or will ever be set up for sale of a single video or series of videos.

An account has to be more valuable than the video files. The account will retain all of it's history, ranking, and reviews for the new owner. If you sell a file, the new owner will have to re-upload and begin from scratch. By selling an account, you should obtain a higher price than selling your videos. You're essentially selling a business instead of an item.

To protect your future choices, try to think about any situations where you might need to have separate accounts.

A second reason you might want multiple accounts is to keep each niche audience separate. For organizational purposes, you might not want to mix quilting videos in with fitness videos. This also sets you up well for any outsourcing. You might eventually hire someone to manage and market all your fitness videos, and they will all be in one place.

Finally, Amazon is known to shut down accounts for violations, and in such cases, it's difficult to get them reopened. If Amazon ever did close one account, then at least your other accounts would still be earning money. Multiple accounts protect your business with multiple streams of income. If one stops, the others keep on going.

Amazon leads you through each step to open an account. Add your personal (Sole Proprietor) or company information, agree to terms, attach a bank account, and complete your tax information.

Account Details

1 COMPLETE YOUR BUSINESS ACCOUNT — About a minute	2 SET UP PAYMENTS FOR YOUR SALES — 3 - 5 minutes	3 SUBMIT YOUR TAX INFORMATION — About 10 minutes

Your Administrator Profile

You will be set up with full control of this business account, and we'll use your contact information below if we need to contact you regarding the account. You can add another administrator at the bottom of this page.

Name
Phone number
Job position   Please choose ⬍

Company Profile

Please enter the primary address where your company currently operates.

Company (What's this?) ▾
Country   Please choose
Address Line 1
Address Line 2 Optional
City
State/Province/Region   Please choose
Postal code
Phone
Email address (What's this?) ▾

Please invite a second administrator who can serve as backup in the event you are unable to access your account.

Name
Email address

Save & Continue

How to Get Started Quickly

Uploading Videos to Amazon Video Direct

If at anytime you need help, Amazon has created an in depth directory of support items. You should open each tab and read through every item to give you an overview of all the requirements. Some of it may not make sense, so revisit this area as your experience level grows.

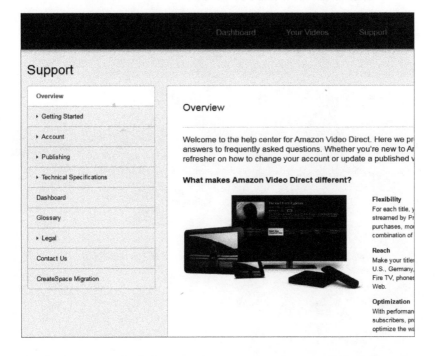

Each option in the left navigation opens to extended choices:

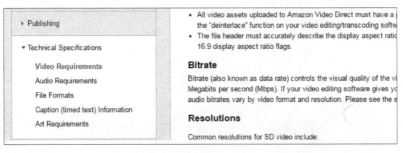

There are three types of uploads:

1. *Standalone videos* - A single video clip, webinar, tutorial, or movie. One video can be as long as 5 hours.

2. *Episodic* - A series of videos that should be viewed in a specific order, such as a course with lesson plans. A series, season, or course tutorial lessons must contain at least 3 videos.

3. *Subscription* - This is a difficult place to start unless you are an experienced videographer. This type takes up to six weeks to go live. It must have a minimum of 30 stand-alone titles or 5 seasons of episodic titles, and must be available for at least 18 months.

Standalone Video

After clicking the Standalone Video tab, click "Add Title"

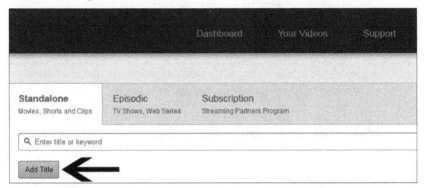

A pop-up box opens and you will enter your Title, Category, and Language.

The language here is "Used for all customer-facing metadata" which refers to the language you are using to submit your data. For example, if your film is in Spanish, but you are submitting your listing using the English language, choose English. These entries are all editable on the next screen. Click continue.

After clicking continue, four topic tabs appear:

1. *Catalog Listing:* Includes everything used to advertise your video on Amazon.com, and these items should also help your listing appear in Google search results.

2. *Cast and Crew:* Contains more items that may help gain exposure of your video in searches on Amazon.com.

3. *Video Assets:* Here you will upload your required video, caption files, and possibly an optional trailer.

4. *Availability:* This is where you select the countries that can view your video, a release date, and your royalty settings.

Catalog Listing Tab

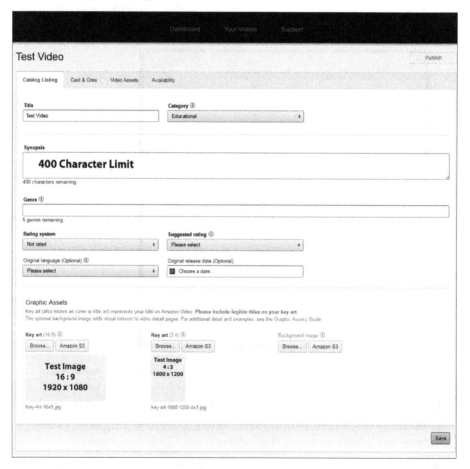

Title

The first entry in your catalog listing is your Title. This field auto fills from the previous pop-up screen, but you can edit it here. In the sample image, the title is "Test Video."

When choosing your title, consider the words from a "search" perspective. This means to think about the words someone might type in a search box to find your title. Try to use these words in this field because it will help your video be found.

Category

The next box is your Category. This is the category where your listing will appear on Amazon.com. Your choices are described under the AVD *Support > Publishing > Change Title Metadata*:

> • *TV Shows:* A segment of content intended for broadcast. Typically, this is episodic content that is part of a series. Examples: Sitcoms, Game Shows, Cartoons, Crime Dramas
>
> • *Short films:* Standalone motion picture content that has a run time of 40 minutes or less. Includes collections of short films. Examples: Comedies, Dramas, Romance, Thrillers
>
> • *Clips:* A short video (run time of five minutes or less) or compilation of short videos. Examples: Excerpts from sports or TV broadcasts, "Best of" complications, highlight reel
>
> • *Concerts:* A performer or group of performers present one or more works of art. Examples: Concerts, musicals, theater, dancing, circus shows, stand-up comedy
>
> • *Educational:* Informative or educational in nature. Examples: How-to, scientific principles, language training, exercise
>
> • *Interviews:* One-on-one or one-to-many conversation with questions and answers. Examples: Cast and crew, celebrity, political interviews
>
> • *Music Videos:* A short film integrating music and imagery. Examples: Band or performer's official music video, music tribute videos

> • *Reporting and Journalism:* News broadcasts, political discussions. Examples: Originally broadcast news programs, reports and updates of current events
>
> • *Reviews:* Evaluation of a product, service, event, or content. Examples: Gadget review or unboxing, book or film critique
>
> • *Sporting Events:* Archived broadcast of a sanctioned sporting event. Examples: Football game, boxing match, golf tournament

Your video might qualify for two categories, but don't worry about that right now. Choose one, upload your video, and get it approved. Later, you can come back and optimize further.

Synopsis

The next entry is the Synopsis of your video. When your goal is to start fast, you might use a very simple description. Don't give Amazon any extra words, any reason to disapprove your uploaded video.

After your video is approved and live, you can come back here to edit and optimize your synopsis using keywords. Keywords and ranking are discussed more in a later section.

Genre

The next entry is Genre. At the time of this writing, Amazon did not have a published list of their Genres, so you have to click in the box and scroll to make your choices. For your convenience, there is a consolidated Genre list in the Resource section of this book to assist you in planning your videos.

You can choose up to five genres, however, to get started fast, choose only one. Add more later. Five genre options should give your listing more opportunities to be found on Amazon, but adding five immediately may also increase the time you wait for video approval. Note that when you do add four more genres and republish, your video status will revert to "processing" but as you wait, your first submission is still "Live" in the initial approved Genre category. It continues to gain views while you wait for your update to be approved.

Rating, Language, and Release Date

• *Rating System:* If your video has been *officially* rated, choose the appropriate option, otherwise, choose Not Rated.

Rating system
Not rated
MPAA - Motion Picture Association of America
TVPG - TV Parental Guidelines
FSK - Freiwillige Selbstkontrolle der Filmwirtschaft
BBFC - British Board of Film Classification
Eirin - Eiga Rinri Kanri Iinkai

• *Suggested Rating:* Choose the appropriate age option. These correspond to the agency you may have chosen under the Rating System. If you chose, "Not Rated" then your choices here will be your *suggested* rating of: all ages, 7+, 13+, or 18+ for your viewing audience. If needed, do some research on acceptable language, nudity, and graphics that would impact your choice.

• *Original Language:* Select the original language used in your video. If your actors or narrator is speaking Spanish, then this is where you would choose Spanish. You can also choose specific dialects here, such as English (United Kingdom) if your actors have an accent.

— Even though this area is optional, the more information you provide, the more Amazon can use to match your listing to search inquiries and target each individual customer's interests.

• *Original Release Date:* If your video was originally shown on another date (such as a date published on YouTube), you might include that here. Amazon does have a left navigation filter to allow customers to sort results by Decade, so this field may help you be found.

Graphic Assets

Your "Key Art" refers to the graphic images that Amazon uses to advertise your video. Amazon states, "Please include legible titles on your Key Art." Your image should contain the exact title of your video, word-for-word. Your Key Art is similar to a book cover or movie poster. The words on this image must match the words used in the Title box.

Remember that Amazon is all about user experience. When you create these images, the closer they can be to "Movie Poster" advertisements, the better your chances are for approval.

Size matters! Your image text should be large enough that it will be readable when displayed in thumbnail size on Amazon search results. Also consider superimposing a Play Button image on top of your graphic art. This may help indicate to users that this image relates to a video and may help you gain more views.

Your images can be in either .jpg or .png format. If you have an error using .png files, try uploading a .jpg version. The first Standalone image is a horizontal landscape format and will be a ratio of 16:9 and should be 1920x1080 pixels. The second Standalone image is a vertical, book style format and uses a ratio of 3:4 and 1200x1600 pixels. These images can be created in your favorite image editing software, such as Photoshop.

Name your video file using some keywords that users might enter to find your video or use the title of your video. For example, you might name your instructional pet health video that applies to both cats and dogs: cat-dog-healthcare-tips.jpg before uploading. If you find better keywords later, you can certainly rename your image, upload a new file, and republish.

Remember to click "Save" before moving on to the next tab.

Cast and Crew Tab

In this section you will list the company or brand and also any people involved in creating your video or film.

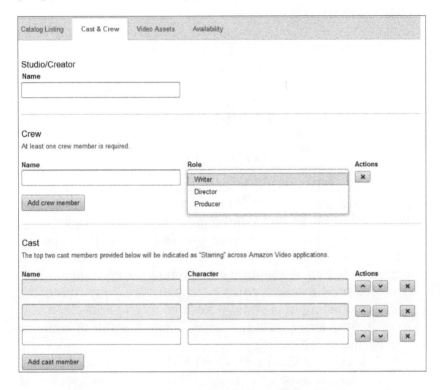

- *Studio / Creator:* You might use your company or brand name here, but if your own name is your brand (such as a celebrity) use your real name.
- *Crew:* This is a place to list your Producer, Director, and Writer. Director and Writer will be clickable links across Amazon pages.
- *Cast:* The top two cast members will be listed as "Starring" and be clickable links across Amazon pages.

Remember to click "Save" before moving on to the next tab.

Video Assets Tab

Under the Video Assets tab, there are three upload options: your video, caption, and trailer files. The first two are required, but the trailer is optional.

Mezzanine file

Browse to your file location to upload your video. For language, choose the language your video is *intended* for. If Italian is spoken with English subtitles burned into the video, choose English.

If you're not a professional videographer, the technical specifications may seem overwhelming. Working with Amazon means you need to pay close attention when rendering your final file.

If you're used to just "letting your software do its thing" or uploading to the Internet straight from your cell phone, then you may be in for a small learning curve. This can result in hours of extreme frustration!

Whether you use Camtasia, Corel Video Studio, Sony Vegas, Adobe Premier, or another software, if in the past, you just clicked through default settings, from now on, you need to actually read all those tech screens to determine what your software is doing. Resolution and Frames Per Second (FPS) are the top things to watch out for.

Resolutions accepted are:

- For SD video include:
  - 640x480 (4:3 aspect ratio)
  - 640x360 (16:9 aspect ratio)
- For HD video include:
  - 1280x720 (16:9 aspect ratio)
  - 1920x1080 (16:9 aspect ratio)

Frames per second accepted are:

> Amazon Video Direct supports the following frame rates: 23.976, 24, 25, 29.97, and 30 frames per second (FPS).

One way to check your files is to go into your file manager, right click on your file, and choose *Properties*. Next, click the *Details Tab* to see your settings. You will immediately see if your resolution and fps settings are acceptable.

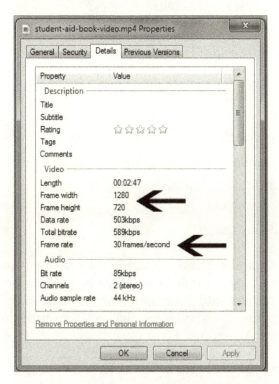

Common errors seem to come from the resolution, frames per second, and file format selected along with corresponding codec. If these terms don't quite make sense to you, begin reading online articles about video creation, or look for a Facebook or local film group that might assist you with video technicalities. Also check the troubleshooting section in this book. It seems that Amazon requires content creators to understand much more about the intricacies of video than other platforms.

Captions

An even bigger issue seems to be the Caption requirement. Since YouTube has spoiled content providers by assisting in creating their video captions, many people expect the same courtesy from Amazon. However, Amazon only offers a list of providers to help create captions:

- 3Play Media
  - http://www.3playmedia.com
- Media Access Group WGBH-TV
  - http://mediaaccessgroupwgbh.org/
- Rev
  - https://www.rev.com
- SubPly
  - http://www.subply.com
- Visual Data Media
  - http://www.visualdatamedia.com
- Vitac
  - http://www.vitac.com

Captions, transcripts, and subtitles generally refer to the same thing: written text of all audio that takes place in your video. Subtitles are usually burned into your film. They are part of the actual video file. Captions are something that you can turn on and off. In addition, per Amazon:

> If a title contains no dialogue or has extended scenes with no spoken content, captions should include a description of the foreground or background audio elements. Extended silent scenes should be captioned with [no audio].

It's possible that Amazon might use caption files in its search algorithm. Keeping this in mind, it's a good idea to include keywords and a verbal *Call to Action* in the audio of every video you create. You might add an introduction or ending to your videos that contain only music. Adding words will allow you to create some quality text for a caption file.

The easiest, cheapest way to create a caption file is to upload your video to YouTube and wait for YouTube to automatically create a caption file. You can upload your video as "Private" if you don't want it to actually appear in YouTube and Google Search results.

You can find YouTube's information on Captions here:
https://support.google.com/youtube/answer/2734796

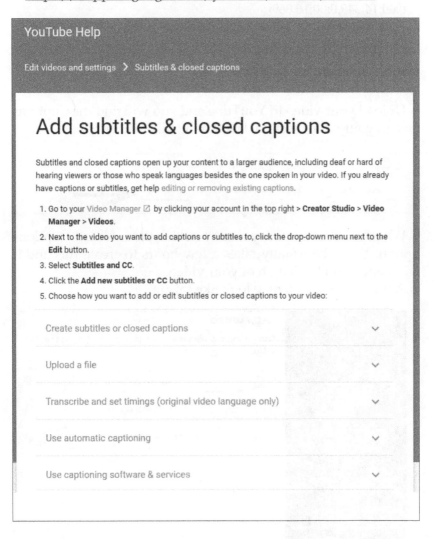

YouTube Help

Edit videos and settings ❯ Subtitles & closed captions

Add subtitles & closed captions

Subtitles and closed captions open up your content to a larger audience, including deaf or hard of hearing viewers or those who speak languages besides the one spoken in your video. If you already have captions or subtitles, get help editing or removing existing captions.

1. Go to your Video Manager ☑ by clicking your account in the top right > **Creator Studio** > **Video Manager** > **Videos**.
2. Next to the video you want to add captions or subtitles to, click the drop-down menu next to the **Edit** button.
3. Select **Subtitles and CC**.
4. Click the **Add new subtitles or CC** button.
5. Choose how you want to add or edit subtitles or closed captions to your video:

Create subtitles or closed captions ⌄

Upload a file ⌄

Transcribe and set timings (original video language only) ⌄

Use automatic captioning ⌄

Use captioning software & services ⌄

A caption file will contain a mixture of time codes and text written similar to this format:

0:00:08.360,0:00:10.030
My beginning text would be here.

0:00:11.219,0:00:14.349
This is text that begins at about 11 seconds into the video.

0:00:14.349,0:00:16.869
This text starts 14.349 seconds and lasts until 16.869 seconds.

Using YouTube for Captions

Upload your video to YouTube and you will find the Captions area in your editor section, last tab called: *Subtitles & CC.*

When you first upload, you may not see the automatic captions option. YouTube usually takes a few hours to create this and it will depend on the length of your video.

At first your screen may look like this:

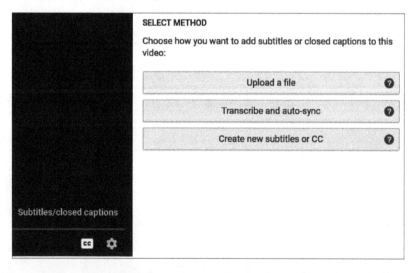

If you don't want to wait for the automatic captions, YouTube gives you these three additional options to create your own, as shown in the prior image.

1. *Upload a file:* Used by YouTube users when they already have a caption file

2. *Transcribe and auto-sync:* Used to type or copy/paste in a complete transcript of the video and YouTube will set the subtitle timings automatically.

   — Use this option if you hired someone to transcribe the audio of your video into a transcript, but they didn't actually create a timed caption file. This can be cheaper than using the caption companies suggested by Amazon Video Direct. If you decide to use this transcript upload method, you would paste in the transcribed text and YouTube will do its best to create the timed caption settings.

3. *Create new subtitles or cc:* Used to manually create subtitles and closed captions by typing them in yourself as you watch your video.

   — This option allows you to play your video and type in the captions yourself. This works well for short videos and creators on a tight budget.

The goal here is to create a file that you can download and use for Amazon Video Direct.

When automatic captions are generated, you'll see Language (Automatic) in the "Published" section to the right of the video. If you began one of the other choices described above, you might also see a Draft option. Both are shown in the next image.

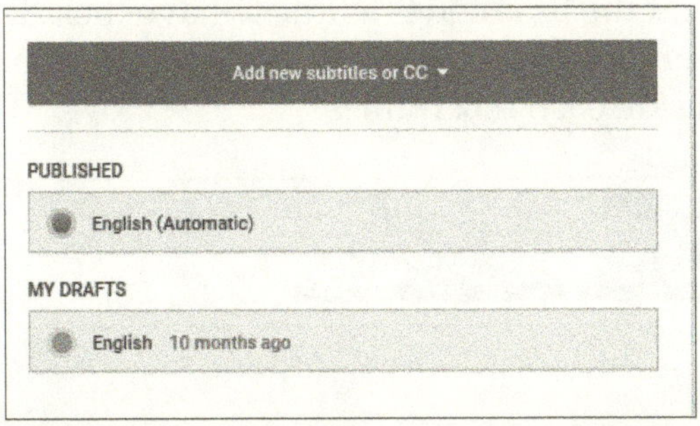

Amazon Video Direct requires a grammatically correct caption file that perfectly time matches your video file. So in all cases, you should check your YouTube caption file before downloading.

The accuracy of an automatic file depends on how well the YouTube text-to-speech software recognizes the pronunciation used within your audio. Most likely, you will need to make corrections. You can also follow these steps to review a file created using the other methods.

Click on the caption file you wish to review and a screen similar to this will appear with your text and times in it:

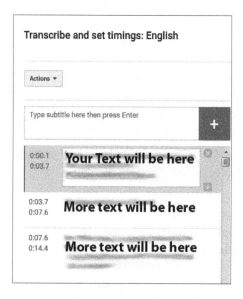

Turn on the captions by clicking the cc located on the lower right of your video (see arrow in the next image) and play your video while reading the text on the screen (see arrow in the next image).

Check that the words are in sync with your audio. In some cases you may need to also edit the time codes a little to have them line up perfectly with the audio voice. Make your spelling, grammar, and time frame edits inside each box frames.

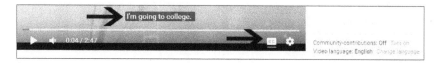

To download your caption file, refresh your page and look for the *Actions* button above your text. This has a drop-down arrow. Click the arrow down and you may see a choice of file options as shown in the next image, or you may just see a download option. For some reason, the download choices seem to vary.

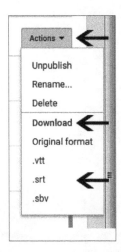

Either way, the goal is to download your file, so look for an option to do this. If you have choices, choose the .srt file, as this format seems to have the most success.

If you have no choices and simply click download. You may find that you downloaded a .sbv file that you need to convert to .srt format. Open the .sbv file in notepad or you can use a free text editor. An excellent free text editor is Crimson Editor found at:
http://www.crimsoneditor.com/

Select all your text from this file and copy/paste it into a converter. A good converter for .sbv to .srt is found at DCMP.org:
http://www.dcmp.org/ciy/converting-youtube-to-srt.html

Follow the steps and copy the output file back into your editor (or notepad) and save as .srt. When saving your file, use keywords that might be used to find your video. If Amazon factors file names into their search algorithms, the caption file name could be important.

Check the ending time code on your .srt file. Make sure this timing matches exactly to the length of your video. If yes, you should have a good caption file to upload.

Remember to click "Save" before moving on to the next tab.

Availability Tab

Catalog Listing	Cast & Crew	Video Assets	Availability	

Where do you have rights for this video? ⓘ
◉ Worldwide
◎ Only in the following countries/regions...

How will Amazon customers watch this video? ⓘ
☑ Included with Prime
☑ Free with Pre-Roll Ad (U.S. only; recommended for short form titles)
☑ Rent
☑ Buy

Which pricing model do you want to use? ⓘ
◉ Preset pricing
◎ Custom pricing (advanced)

Pricing model

	Base Best for balancing cost with wide audience appeal		Value Best for older or back catalog videos	
HD	**Rent**	**Buy**	**Rent**	**Buy**
Amazon.com	$2.99	$9.99	$1.99	$4.99
Amazon.co.uk	£4.49	£9.99	£3.49	£7.99
Amazon.de	€4.99	€11.99	€3.99	€9.99
Amazon.co.jp	¥200	¥1000	¥100	¥500
SD	**Rent**	**Buy**	**Rent**	**Buy**
Amazon.com	$1.99	$7.99	$0.99	$2.99
Amazon.co.uk	£3.49	£7.99	£2.49	£6.99
Amazon.de	€3.99	€9.99	€2.99	€7.99
Amazon.co.jp	¥200	¥1000	¥100	¥500

When should this video be available? ⓘ
◉ As soon as possible
◎ On a specific date
◎ Advanced options

You might reread the previous discussion on monetization ideas before you decide on your royalty options.

If you turn on the options to Rent and Buy, you will have two choices of pricing:

- *Preset Pricing:* This is illustrated in the prior image and has two choices:
  - *Base:* Usually used for new releases, new content
  - *Value:* Usually used for older videos or if you want to offer the cheapest price possible

- *Custom Pricing:* This is shown in the next image. You have options to set your own price for SD and HD. Rental prices typically range between $3.99-$5.99, with SD being a little cheaper. Purchase prices usually range from $9.99 to $14.99 for movies. Courses or lengthy tutorials might be priced higher.

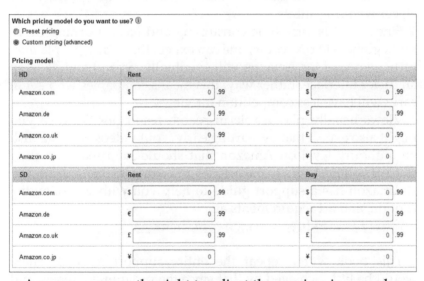

Which pricing model do you want to use? ⓘ
◉ Preset pricing
◉ Custom pricing (advanced)

Pricing model

HD	Rent				Buy			
Amazon.com	$		0	.99	$		0	.99
Amazon.de	€		0	.99	€		0	.99
Amazon.co.uk	£		0	.99	£		0	.99
Amazon.co.jp	¥		0		¥		0	
SD	**Rent**				**Buy**			
Amazon.com	$		0	.99	$		0	.99
Amazon.de	€		0	.99	€		0	.99
Amazon.co.uk	£		0	.99	£		0	.99
Amazon.co.jp	¥		0		¥		0	

Amazon reserves the right to adjust these prices in accordance with typical films and to keep your video priced competitively, so don't price your ten minute video at $49.99.

When you've made your decision, the final step is to click "Save." You should have four check marks, so click Publish!

✓ Catalog Listing	✓ Cast & Crew	✓ Video Assets	✓ Availability

Roadblocks and Troubleshooting

If you are not a film producer or experienced videographer, you may find the Amazon support section feels like you're reading instructions in a foreign language.

This complexity will discourage creators from using Amazon Video Direct. In fact, there are already a ton of videos on YouTube criticizing Amazon Video Direct and complaining about how un-user friendly it is.

Perhaps Amazon's strict policy will result in higher quality videos and provide a better viewer experience. Amazon may gain a reputation of being more professional and perhaps be more educational when compared to YouTube. Amazon seems to want to compete with the tutorial courses found on Udemy and the higher professional filmmaking found on Vimeo and Netflix. Amazon customers may never be exposed to cute cat videos or clever wedding stunts.

Since AVD is very time consuming and has a learning curve for beginners to overcome, one can expect that many people may turn away and/or Amazon will eventually expand and develop an easier interface. Either way, this means companies who get in early will have less competition for views.

Views usually play a role in search result positions, so you might also expect that by starting early, your videos will establish an authority level on Amazon that should help maintain their status as others begin to participate and compete on the platform.

Amazon has a support guide to help you with video, audio, caption, and art requirements at:
https://videodirect.amazon.com/home/help

This book won't repeat the entire support manual. There would be little achieved by that since the program is so new and you should expect many small adjustments over the next year. Content creators should make it a common practice to skim the help section often to check for updates, changes, and new features.

New User Questions

Here are some initial questions and answers to help with your decision to use Amazon Video Direct, as well as some stumbling blocks you might run into when first uploading:

1. Will the Amazon Video play in every browser?

    — It plays quickly in Opera and Chrome. Mozilla Firefox was a little slow and you have to have Silverlight activated. For Apple devices such as the iPad and iPhone, users should download the free Amazon Video app.

2. Will an Amazon Video URL be indexed in Google?

    — Yes. It's just like any other Internet URL.

3. Can I load a .srt file a for Captions?

    — Yes

4. Can I see some sample videos that people have uploaded on Amazon, so I can see how they look?

    — Yes, go here:
    https://www.amazon.com/financial-aid/dp/B01FYRS8FM/

5. If I upload a new video to update information, will my video keep the same URL on Amazon and thus, retain all past authority to rank well on both Amazon and Google?

    — Yes

6. Can I preview a video listing after approval but before it goes live?

    — No

7. When will my uploaded video go live?

    — You set this under the Availability tab. The option, *As Soon As Possible* means your video will go live immediately after approval. If you set a date in the future, your video goes live on that date. Keep in mind that approval takes time. It can take anywhere from 24 hours to 2 weeks for approval.

8. How do I delete a video?

   — Here's the answer from Amazon support:

   > "Currently there is not a way to delete titles from your account. If your video is available on Amazon, you can remove the availability. To take a video offer down from Amazon, you'll need to make your video unavailable for sale. Here's how:
   >
   > 1. Go to Your Videos and click on the video content you'd like to take down.
   >
   > 2. Click the Availability tab.
   >
   > 3. Select Advanced options under "When should this video be available?"
   >
   > 4. Click "Edit" under the end date of each market-place you'd like to remove your video offer from.
   >
   > 5. Change the end date to yesterday's date for each applicable marketplace.
   >
   > 6. Click "Save" and "Publish."
   >
   > You will still be able to see your video title under Your Videos in case you decide to make it available for sale again."

9. Can you continue to make edits after approval?

   — Yes, but your video will go through the approval process again, and the original video remains live until the new one is approved.

Uploading and Troubleshooting Errors

The following are errors you might encounter:

1. *Caption Format:* When I downloaded my captions from a YouTube video, my only choice was a .sbv file. How do I create or convert .sbv to .srt?

   — Try converting from .sbv to .srt at DCMP.org: dcmp.org/ciy/converting-youtube-to-srt.html

2. *Time Out Error:* "Your files could not be uploaded at this time. Please try again"

   — Possible Solutions: Your server was slow, try again now or at a different time of day. You might also try another browser or try uploading a different file type such as .mp4 instead of .mov.

3. *Captions:* "Captions are required for all titles published in the U.S. and Amazon Prime titles worldwide, except Japan."

   — Possible Solution: Create and add captions or try to fix your caption file.

4. *Timed Text:* "An error occurred while processing the timed text file. This file won't successfully complete the encoding workflows. Please submit a new file."

   — Possible Solution: Try uploading a different file format, and also check that the caption time length matches the video length exactly.

5. *Key Art:* "We are unable to publish your title for the following reason(s): The Key Art contains content which violates our Content Policy Guidelines."

   — Possible Solution: Check that your Key Art has the exact Title. Also, check rules at Amazon *Support > Legal > Content Policy Guidelines.*

6. *Image:* "Image has incorrect aspect ratio"

   — Possible Solution: Double check your ratios. Also try uploading a .jpg image instead of .png.

7. *Frame Rate:* "The source file's video frame rate is invalid. A frame rate of 23.98, 24.0, 25.0, 29.97 or 30.0 fps is required. Please submit a new file."

   — Possible Solutions: Check that the video length exactly matches the caption length. Check your FPS, especially for Camtasia 7 users, since the software defaults to recording at 15fps. (Check a file by going to *File Manager,* right click on your file, choose *Properties* and look under the *Details Tab.*)

8. *Codec:* "The source file's extension is incompatible with the video codec. Make sure .mov files have a ProRes 422 HQ video codec and .mp4, .m2t and .TS files have an AVC or H.264 video codec. Please submit a new file."

   — Possible Solution: Did you upload a .mov file with a H.264 codec? Try uploading .mp4 format.

9. *Captions - Poor Customer Experience:* "We are unable to publish your title for the following reason(s): The captions/timed-text contains content which violates our Content Policy Guidelines, specifically, the section regarding Poor Customer Experience."

   — Possible Solution: Check that the caption length matches video length – exactly. Also, check your Key Art images. Are they high quality, attractive, user enticing images? Does the Title of your Video appear word-for-word on the image? If you can't solve it on your own, contact Customer Service.

10. *Mezzanine File - Poor Customer Experience:* "The mezzanine file contains content which violates our Content Guidelines, specifically, the section regarding Poor Customer Experience"

    — Possible Solution: This is the worst error notification because you are left to guess what the issue might be and if it's fixable or if Amazon is just rejecting your content. Read the guidelines again for ideas, contact customer support, or decide that Amazon just doesn't want this video and move on to your next upload.

Goals & Conversions

Your Video Marketing Objectives

You may have many goals when using Amazon Video Direct. Some of your objectives might be:

1. *Monetization:* Earn income through either the ad system or people renting/buying your videos on Amazon.

2. *Product Exposure:* Use your video to highlight a product already on Amazon or another site.

3. *Discovery and Brand Exposure:* Help people find your business or discover you, if you are your business.

4. *Leads or List Building Traffic:* Create a video that entices the viewer to seek out your product or service and/or to sign up for your mailing list.

5. *Serving Others:* This includes educational videos and perhaps videos for a cause (politics, charity, etc.).

Implicit Calls to Action

Be careful how you implement your Calls to Action (CTAs). The focus of your video should be 100% on the customer experience. Brainstorm ways of showing off your product. Could you make a tutorial about using your handsaw to cut down a Christmas tree or a special jack your company sells that's perfect to change a car tire? Authors could read a chapter from a book. If you sell photography gear, you might create instructional videos using reflectors, green screens, or apps.

Try to keep your CTA subtle. Any highlights or credits should generally appear as a short introduction or toward the end. They should be professionally done, and the goal would be to inspire the viewer to look further for your product or service.

Monetization and Advertising Questions

The following are marketing questions to consider when planning your best approach to using Amazon Video Direct:

1. When will I be paid?

   — In 90 days.

2. Can I put a clickable link in my synopsis description on Amazon?

   — No

3. Can I put my brand URL or my Amazon product URL in my synopsis description, even if I understand it will not be a clickable link?

   — No

4. If I choose "Free with Pre-Roll Ad (U.S. only; recommended for short form titles)," what will the ads look like?

   — A short video clip, the full size of the screen will appear before your video starts to play.

5. If I post a tutorial video for rent/purchase, can I update this video at a later date with a new one so past customers can have the latest information at no extra charge?

   — For customers who rented your video, they will need to either rent it again or purchase it to own it. For customers who purchased the content, they'll be able to access the updated video at any time, including if you choose to have the video unpublished.

6. Can I run an Amazon add for my video and use a Pay Per Click (PPC) option to obtain more user views?

   — Not at this time.

7. Can I create video ads for products I have on places like Kindle, Createspace, or Seller Central to place before my own or other people's videos?

   — Not as of today.

8. Can you embed an Amazon video on another website to increase views and give it more authority?

   — Not at this time.

9. Will the content creator have a "channel" or dedicated URL to show all videos by that person, company, or brand?

   — Sort of... The name of the "Starring" person will be linked to all videos for that "Star" and also your designated "Director" and "Writer" are clickable links. The landing pages for these links could be used for publicity and marketing on social media and other websites.

10. If I upload an Episodic Series that is a course or lesson plan, can I insert a new video later?

    — You cannot insert a video into a published Season, but you can add another Season to a Series. However, there may be a work-around solution. You could upload a new video into an already published Episode slot, and then, edit the Title and Synopsis to reflect the updated content.

11. Can I hide a video until the entire season is uploaded and approved?

    — Yes. You can set your video to be available on a date in the future, and try to have your entire series uploaded and approved before the future "live" date.

12. What image appears if I share my Amazon video URL on Facebook?

    — A form of your Key Art 1200×1600 pixel image. The image size varies whether you use the *Share* button from the Amazon page versus if you copy/ paste the browser URL into a post. Sharing direct from Amazon seems to post the best image and text selection, but is also time consuming. You might consider using the URL method, along with a social media auto-posting software that you can schedule to post and re-post on a regular basis.

Let's Optimize and Rank!

Here is an example of published video. When the user clicks on a link in the search results, they are taken to a page like this:

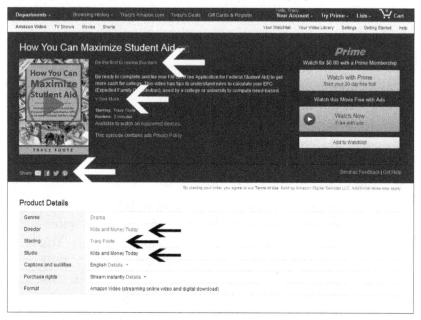

Here's what you might take notice of:

• *Reviews:* There is a place up top to click and leave a review: "Be the first to review this item."

• *Synopsis has See More:* You have to click "See More" to view the entire video synopsis, your entire description.

• *Share:* There are Share buttons to social media on the left hand side, below your Key Art image.

• *Clickable Links:* Under product details, Genre, Director and Starring are all clickable links.

• *Studio/Creator:* Studio is set in your setup under *Cast and Crew* and while it is not clickable, it is still an opportunity for some visual brand exposure. Amazon customers can see this field on the page.

Amazon frequently changes item display pages, so it's a good idea to check back often to monitor your listings.

Identify Your Keywords

The most important factor in ranking is *conversions*. But you can't convert without being found, so you need to first optimize your listing.

You can begin by learning how your target audience searches. The words a they type into the Amazon Search Box are called *Search Terms*. The core words about your product are referred to as *Keywords*. Sometimes, search terms and keywords can be the same thing.

When users type in their search terms, you want your video to appear on page one of the displayed results, preferably in the top position.

You optimize your listing by including keywords and search terms in your Title, Synopsis and file names used for your Key Art, Mezzanine, captions, and trailer. If your keyword is also a word on the Genre list, then you could also choose that Genre as one of your five choices. The full Genre list is provided in the back of this book.

Long-tail Keyword Ideas

As you research your keywords, consider phrases. This group of keywords is referred to as long-tail keywords. Examples might include buying keywords (such as the word buy or best), local keywords (like your city name), informational keywords (learn, advice, secrets), words related to self-improvement or tutorials, and inspirational or emotional keywords. Emotional keywords can help with conversions. Do you want party favors or fun party favors? Try using long-tail phrases to reach more viewers.

Don't forget about Google too! Adding long-tail keywords may also help you rank well in Google's search results. Here are some words you might add to the end of your niche or topic keywords:

- Video, online video, film
- Year (the current year)
- Location (your city, town, state, country)
- Buy, purchase, for sale, for rent, best
- Review, unboxing, tutorial, course, class
- How to, help, information, tip, idea

Title

Historically, Amazon has given weight to the words used first in a title, so try to begin your title with your primary, most important keyword. The first word is thought to count the most (have the most relevance), followed by the second, third, and so on, in a sort of weighed algorithm. A short three word title means the weight value is spread across three words. A ten word title spreads the weight across ten words. In both cases, your first word receives the most weight or points toward ranking, and each word after receives less than the one prior.

You can also work long-tail keywords into your Title. These should have less competition than your primary keywords, and may help you get views faster. Since you can update your video, you might start with a long-tail title and later, after your listing has built some authority, switch to a more competitive title.

Synopsis

You will also use your main keywords towards the front of your synopsis. This field has a 400 character limit, so work in MS Word or another program to count the characters you plan to use.

The first 210 characters appear immediately. The user has to click "See More" to view your entire synopsis, so be sure your first sentence not only has keywords, but encourages the user to click through and watch. Perhaps, state the problem you solve or the entertainment you will provide. You might even have your sentence purposely break off which may entice the user to click "See More" in order to finish reading.

Here is an example of how "See More" is displayed on Amazon:

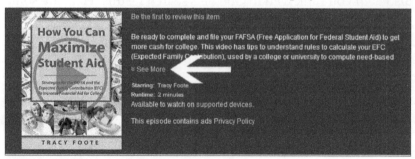

One Keyword Phrase per Video

One ranking strategy you might try is to target one keyword or long-tail phrase per video, usually done with a short video.

Suppose you have three videos on tourist information for New York. You might create one video focused on the keyword phrase "New York travel," another on "New York trip," and a third on "New York vacation."

A common mistake is to add these phrases to all three videos. If you did include the same phrase on all three videos, it's like placing all three videos in a hat and asking Amazon to pick one for "New York trip." All three videos compete against each other. Amazon will choose the best video for "New York trip," so each video has a one in three chance of being selected for spot number one in the search results.

A better strategy is to avoid duplication and have a unique focus for each video. You are simulating being the one video in the hat when Amazon (or Google Search) pulls a result. You say, "No need to guess. This is the video to rank for this term."

Of course, this practices only eliminates competing against yourself. You still have to beat out the other competitors for that keyword term and that number one position in results. You still need to indicate that your video is more relevant than any others for your targeted keywords, the best choice to present to Amazon customers.

Focusing on one keyword phrase is a challenge for lengthy films. How will they compete for a phrase like "Horror film" if there are 1,000 such films listed on Amazon? The answer is to rank for longer keyword phrases and grow your views and reviews so that Amazon will see you as relevant for the more general phrase.

Keyword Research

Before you can rank for your keywords, you have to identify them. In the back of this book, under Resources, you'll find websites you can use for keyword research. Spend some time and choose the best keywords for your film or video. This should help you rank well on both Amazon and in Google's organic search results.

Look for the best keywords to pull in your desired amount of targeted traffic. Words that have a high number of users searching for them indicates that these words are popular and have high demand. A high number of searches will transition into traffic, and with more traffic, you should have more conversion opportunities.

Watch for targeted low traffic words as well. They will have less competition and should be easy to rank for. Even though these words may only bring an occasional conversion, such as: once a month or even quarterly, you may was well grab them too.

Make a list of all your keywords, including long-tail keywords. If you do this prior to filming, you will find it easier to create high converting videos, because you are creating what the customer wants. You've already confirmed a demand for your video.

Evaluate Your Competition

To evaluate the competition, use a spreadsheet like this one:

Keyword	# of Searches	# Videos on Amazon	# of Reviews for top video
horror film	10,000	10,143	44
scary film	12,000	1,000	2
fright film	40,000	9,000	50

Place your keywords in the first column of the spreadsheet and next to that, create a column to record the number of searches for that keyword. (The number of searches comes from whatever tool you used for keyword research.)

Next, go to Amazon. Type your keyword into the search box, and use the arrow drop-down tab to filter by Amazon Video.

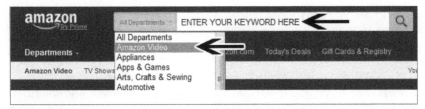

Observe and record the number of videos that currently exist for that keyword. These are your competitors. These are the videos that your video will compete with for position on Amazon.

In the next image, there are 10,143 videos ranking for the term "horror film" and only 40 are offering to view "Free with Ads."

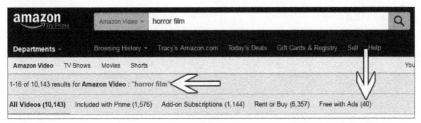

Run this search for each of your keywords and record the number of existing videos onto your spreadsheet in column three.

In the fourth column, record the highest number of reviews that any video in this category had. At the time of this writing, one horror film had 44 reviews, so you'd enter 44 in column four.

You might add more columns to track the royalty options: Prime, Rent, Buy, and Ads. You can use your spreadsheet to:

- Prioritize what video and keywords to focus on first, based on the demand and competition.

- Develop a realistic expectation of how soon your video might rank in the top positions on Amazon. (If there are only two videos, you should rank quickly.)

- Predict the potential traffic your video might generate based on the user engagement (indicated by the current number of reviews posted to similar niche videos).

Note that if you did not use the drop-down filter, the results would show how ALL items on Amazon rank for this keyword, not just those in Video. You should first focus on ranking well in the video subcategory. Later, you can expand, create a spreadsheet for all Amazon products, and take your video to the next level by trying to rank first amongst all Amazon products.

Using Filters to Fine Tune Your Listing

You can try to use the left navigation options to help with keyword research and gather ideas to fine tune your videos.

Purchase Type (first arrow in the image below) shows how many videos using your keyword are offered as Rentals and Purchases. This should help when choosing your royalty settings. If everyone on Amazon is offering rentals and no purchases, you should follow the trend to keep your video competitive.

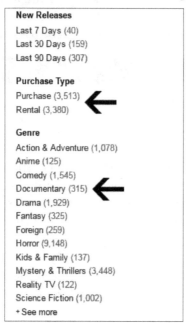

The second arrow shows the number of videos in each Genre. It should be easier to rank a horror film in *Documentary* and compete against 315 videos, versus *Mystery & Thrillers* where you compete against 3,448. Click "See More" to reveal the full list to make a good decision.

Action & Adventure (1,074)	Horror (9,133)	Romance (110)
Anime (125)	Kids & Family (150)	Science Fiction (1,014)
Bollywood (21)	LGBT (110)	Soap Operas (41)
Comedy (1,527)	Military & War (107)	Special Interests (66)
Documentary (311)	Music Videos & Concerts (58) 58)	Sports (3)
Drama (1,904)	Musicals (62)	TV Game Shows (9)
Exercise & Fitness (1)	Mystery & Thrillers (3,425)	TV News Programming (7)
Fantasy (325)	Performing Arts (29)	TV Talk Shows (17)
Foreign (259)	Reality TV (120)	Westerns (40)

If your videos fall into two genres, this navigation information may also help you choose one over another. You might add more columns to your previous spreadsheet to track Genres if it will help with your decision process.

More Keyword Research Ideas

1. *Brainstorm:* Make a target audience(s) list and research a list of search terms you think they might use.

2. *Amazon Search Box*: Start typing your keywords into the Amazon search box and record the suggestions Amazon automatically creates as you type. You can even type in your keyword with each letter of the alphabet to see what amazon suggests. For example, type in: Horror a, then: Horror b, next: Horror c, and so on to trigger Amazon to suggest a follow-on word that begins with a, b, c, and so forth.

3. *Google AdWords Keyword Tool*: Use the *Phrase Search* at http://www.AdWords.Google.com/o/KeywordTool and choose keywords with at least 10,000 monthly searches. (Don't worry about the competition column.)

4. *Call-to-Action Words*: Make a list of words related to your *Calls to Action*. This might include problem solving words like: purchase, buy, how to, help, tutorial, and so forth. Combine these with other keywords on your list.

5. *Frequently Asked Questions (FAQs)*: Make a list of keywords associated with the question most frequently asked by your customer.

6. *Trend Observation:* You can research the type of videos that are currently ranking. What are the leaders in your niche focused on? What products are popular on Amazon right now or what are people discussing in product reviews? Check this same type of information on Google+, Facebook, Twitter search, Yahoo Answers, niche forums, Pinterest, Yelp, YouTube, and other social networks.

Take Advantage of Clickable Links

In your video set up, under *Cast and Crew* you have two opportunities for extended exposure using clickable links.

Cast - Starring

The *Starring* option creates a clickable link on the Amazon search result page as shown in the next image:

Currently, when the search result is for *"All Departments"* as indicated by the white arrow above, and the user clicks the *Starring* link, the user is shown ALL items on Amazon related to this person as shown here:

Amazon support has said this is expected to change. The coding will be updated so the *Starring* link clicks only to *videos* related to the *Star,* so this added exposure may be temporary for authors.

When the drop-down filter is used in the Search box, the results are different because now, the user has indicated to show only results in a subcategory. When a user filters by *Video* and then clicks the *Starring* link, only video results display. You no longer see other products related to the *Star*. The books are gone.

If the coding is fixed, then these video results will also be what is displayed for an *"All Department"* search. Authors will no longer get the added exposure. Even if changed, everyone can still take advantage of this feature when planning videos. You will always be able to link several videos together by using the *Star* option in the back-end.

Role - Writer, Director, and Producer

The second clickable link is for "Director." This link takes the user to all the films or movies by that director. This is a good place for your company name. You might also use this field to tie a niche group of videos together. Suppose your business is about pets. You could have a sub-brand for cat, dogs, birds and so on. Enter your main brand here with a dash to the subcategory, such as Jane's Pets - Cats and Jane's Pets - Dogs, and now, when the link is clicked, the videos related to each type of pet would show.

The "Writer" option will also create a clickable link, but at the time of this writing, the "Producer" choice does not. This may be a glitch and perhaps become clickable in the future.

To gain more exposure, you might try to use different words in these fields. Don't list yourself as both *Starring* and *Writer*. You might also think about joint ventures. Team up with other creators and have them star in your video to tie your video to theirs on Amazon. Your star could be leaders from social media networks, actors, authors, photographers, fashion designers, or anyone else that might eventually have a listing on Amazon.

Category Keyword Research

Add a keyword (in this example: Student Aid) to your Amazon search box and use the drop-down to select Amazon Video.

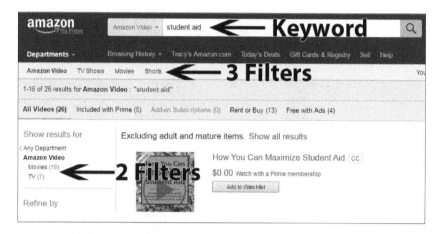

The left navigation shows two Departments for Movie or TV (number 2 in the image). There is also a horizontal navigation that shows TV Shows and Movies, plus an additional category of Shorts. These items happen to be the first three category choices offered in setup, as shown in the next image:

The question arises as to what is better for optimization. Should you select one of the first three general categories or a more niche category such as Education?

You can filter this search by clicking each of the three options: TV, Movie, and Shorts and observe in which subcategory did Amazon placed the video. It was found under Movie.

However, observing all three subcategories also revealed 11 videos related to "Student Aid" listed under Shorts (as illustrated in the next image, first arrow). One might conclude that content creators should place "Student Aid" videos under Shorts versus Education. There is no proven best choice at this time, but this is one way you can use categories to observe, test, and possibly make adjustments to your listings.

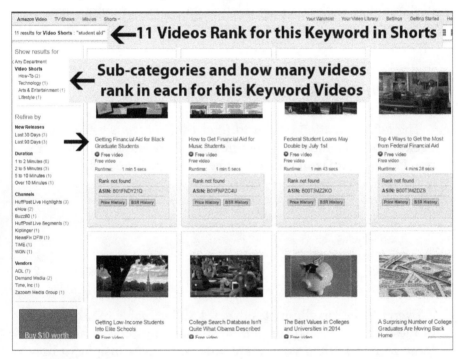

The navigation also shows some detailed subcategory listings (second arrow) and the number of videos in each. This provides ideas for keywords to include in a synopsis (words such as How-to or Technology), plus words to look for in Genre choices.

The final arrow in the image brings attention to the 11 ranking videos. They give ideas for optimization. Write down keywords used in their titles and click through to read and collect more word ideas from their descriptions. The easiest way to do research is to observe what others are already doing that works well and copy this. You might add any newly discovered words to your listing.

If your video qualifies for two categories, spend some time on Amazon browsing each category to get a feel for the target audience. Also, consider the activity in a category. Which has more reviews? This indicates active customers who watch and engage with the page. Amazon likes user interaction. Every review should count as a nudge to rank your video higher in Amazon search results.

Consider competition in a category. How many videos cover the topic? If one category has 100 videos and another has 15, the latter should be easier to rank in. Your video only has to be the best out of 15 to show up on the first page in slot number one.

Your category is another area that you can test, fine tune, and optimize for better results.

Best Duration Time for Your Video

The left navigation option to filter by *Duration* seems to play peek-a-boo on Amazon. Sometimes it's there and other times it's not. Perhaps Amazon is testing whether to include this.

> **Duration**
>
> 1 to 2 Minutes (6)
>
> 2 to 5 Minutes (3)
>
> 5 to 10 Minutes (1)
>
> Over 10 Minutes (1)

Even if Amazon eliminates this, it's still valuable to take notice of these cut-off times Amazon has tentatively chosen, and keep these in mind when you create videos. It gives insight to how Amazon is thinking.

For example, there's not much point in making a video that runs 2.05 minutes, because that length will just miss a filtering cut-off time. Also, once your video extends over two minutes, it's fine to continue producing for up to five minutes without losing any filtering opportunities.

A final thought on video duration is to consider the length of competitor videos. If all competitor videos are under 5 minutes, it's probably not a good idea to create a 30 minute video.

Plan for a High Retention Rate

Retention refers to how much of your video is actually watched in a single sitting before the viewer clicks away. Do most people exit after 30 seconds or do they watch the entire five minutes?

This factor is used by YouTube in their ranking algorithm. It's sometimes called the *viewer retention score*. It's logical that Amazon might also use retention rate as a factor to rank videos, so you may as well plan for this consideration.

As you think about retention rate, your goal should be to entice viewers to watch through to the end, not skipping ahead. This can be done simply by creating an intriguing video, but also by creating teasers. At the beginning of your video, you could state that you'll teach five concepts. This lets the viewer know to watch until number five is reached. You could also announce that you will show something special at the end or what your goal is if you are solving a problem. Viewers will watch through, waiting for that final idea. Another strategy is to include bloopers at the end. As viewers begin to expect these from your brand, they stay tuned, waiting for the funny ending. You are in fact, training them to watch to the end.

The length of your video also plays a role in your watch rate. It's easier for viewers to watch shorter videos to the end because time flies quickly. For this reason, you might aim for short videos. A short video is under 2 minutes in accordance with Amazon's filtering options.

As you think about your retention rate, consider the structure of your video. A popular format used to compel a viewer to complete a *Call to Action* is the sandwich approach. This means you will have some sort of introduction, a middle, and a closure.

Your video outline might look something like this:

- 6-10 second attention grabber
- 5-10 second topic introduction (introduce the context, explain what's coming; convince the viewer to watch)
- 1-2 minute content
- 5-10 second *Call to Action* closure
- 6-10 second credits (brand ending or outtake)

When you begin making films or videos, try to look at movies, TV shows, and advertisements in a different light. What catches your eye? What makes you watch the entire show or ad? Try to implement these tactics into your video to achieve a higher retention rate.

One of the great things about Amazon Video Direct is you can update a video and it keeps the same URL listing. This means you keep your reviews and Amazon knows exactly how many people watched it previously. Amazon doesn't yet provide you with data information as to when in your video a viewer clicks away. This is called a drop-off point. If this is ever provided, you could upload new videos making a slight adjustment at that point in video. Watch for this as AVD evolves and adds new features.

Impact of Age and Freshness

The age of your video may also play a role in ranking. Google uses it, so it's possible Amazon will follow a similar path. Google loves new content. When you first upload a video, it has a high level of *freshness*. It's brand new. You get some *kudos* points for adding fresh Internet material that customers might want. It is fairly easy to initially rank high while Google figures out what type of audience is interested in your video. Your keywords are an indication, but Google *proves* they are correct by using the viewer as the ultimate judge. Customer clicks, or lack there of, will indicate if your video is relevant for a search term.

If Amazon follows a similar practice, you can expect Amazon to test your video for random versions of a keyword, and you will move higher in the rankings as you achieve click-throughs and lower if you're ignored. Because of this, your Key Art and synopsis play a critical role in ranking.

Ironically, you can also receive some *kudos* points for being old. When you've been doing something for a long time, you are viewed as having experience, authority, and credibility. Website domains established since 1999 are valued for their *age*. This age factor can nudge them higher in search result positions.

So IF your video converts well for your chosen keywords, you are slowly building your "age" authority at the same time. When a year from now, someone creates a similar video, it should be difficult for them to bump you out of your ranked position. This is also another reason why it's good to be one of the initial users of Amazon Video Direct. You will be a step ahead of competitors when it comes to the age factor.

Another concept regarding the term age is *premier*. It helps to be the first video on a subject. Google Search will usually rank the original posting of content higher than any duplicate posting.

If Amazon follows suit, you will want to create the first tutorial, present the first review, or be first to break a newsworthy topic. This should give you a nudge forward to rank above later videos.

What weighs more: freshness or age? Suppose there are already six videos on a topic, and you post a new one. Initially, you will probably receive a freshness boost and could even outrank the other videos. But, you are also duplicate content. The oldest posting may still outrank you, especially if it has numerous views and five star reviews. As all seven videos become "old," the other ranking factors (views, watch time, reviews, and whatever else Amazon considers) should kick in, and positions may shift. To hold a position, you need to do more than post fresh content.

Be Evergreen

For the best Return on Investment (ROI), you want to create what is called *Evergreen* videos. Like an evergreen tree, you want your message to stay green throughout every season of the year and for the years to come.

For this reason, you want to avoid placing dates and deadlines within the video footage and audio. You can, and should, put the year in your Title and Synopsis. Each year, simply change these areas to the current year and re-publish. Your video stays relevant with all its history of views and reviews.

Encourage Reviews

Amazon loves reviews. They help with conversions and they are an indication of user activity; user engagement with your listing. In fact, even a bad review can nudge you ahead of someone with no review. A bad review still shows that the user was emotionally connected and passionate enough to make a comment. So don't worry if you receive a poor review. Just focus on more positive ones. You can try to increase your positive reviews by:

1. *Connecting Emotionally:* Create videos that make an emotional connection with viewers so they are more likely to leave a review.

2. *Responding:* Some users think it is a good idea for creators to respond to reviews, perhaps to give an explanation if someone complained or to address a question. Consider your return on time invested. Would your time be better spent making more videos? Will responding help increase your viewer engagement? Maybe a response will inspire another comment, especially with a controversial subject. Will responding set a precedent where all reviewers will now expect you to reply, and do you have time to dedicate to this? These are some thoughts to consider when deciding to respond.

3. *Ask in Your Video*: The obvious is almost never done. Simply ask at the end of your film or video, "If you would rate this 5 stars, please consider leaving a review."

4. *Newsletters*: Add a note at the end of your monthly electronic newsletter, "If you watched our video and think it deserves 5 stars, please leave a review on Amazon. Here's the link: [put your link here]"

5. *Old Fashioned Ads:* If you hand out any flyers or business cards, add a link to watch the video on Amazon and leave a review.

Note: Amazon does not like fake reviews. Amazon will know if a user watched the entire film or video, so don't solicit fake reviews.

Increase Views

A view, whether free or paid, equates to a conversion, and these conversions will boost your ranking position in search results. You want to do all you can to increase views.

If you have any traditional marketing materials, such as a catalog or flyer, consider adding your Amazon Video Direct URLs on these documents. When your customer receives a flyer, it could invite them to watch an online tutorial on Amazon.com. Your cost is only the cost of the additional ink, because you are adding this to marketing you already pay for.

If you have a website (even if it's a single sales page), you might brainstorm ways of bringing that customer to Amazon. Perhaps when a customer completes an opt-in form, you might add an Amazon link in your *Thank You Confirmation* e-mail.

Some may argue that ultimately a business should aim to bring customers to their website or retail store, so why send a user over to Amazon? First, most businesses grow when they focus on the *user experience*, so if the video will help your user — send them to Amazon. Second, you want to create a balance between Amazon and your company. By sending your customer to Amazon, you are helping your video reach even more new customers. It's a win-win situation. This additional Amazon traffic will increase your views and boost your listing's position. The goal is to tap into the Amazon audience.

If you sell a product, you might make a product review video, but you can also make a video that tells a story that features your product. This might be more entertaining and pull more views. The same concept can be applied to a service. Think of all the items you see in at the cinema today. When you see a brand in a film, it was not placed there by accident. There's a reason the actor drinks a certain soda or uses a specific detergent when doing laundry. Perhaps your film will have the actor call a particular plumber in a specific city (if you offer plumbing services). There's a lot of room for creativity.

Connect to Other Related Items

Think about your target audience. What else do they search for on Amazon that is related to your video? Amazon promotes related products together, so a goal should be to have your videos listed on as many pages as possible — as a related product. Related products often appear on *product pages* under headings like "Frequently Bought Together" or "Customers Who Bought this Item Also Bought." On *video pages*, the heading is "Customers Who Watched This Item Also Watched" as in this dog example:

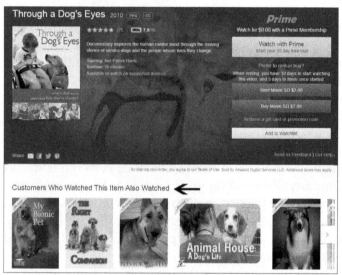

It should be easier to first try to connect with other videos in your category vs. other products on Amazon, because the creators have already designated these videos as similar to yours. You can trigger a relationship by watching your video and then watching the video you wish to connect to. One view is probably not enough though, so to get more related views, share both videos (yours and theirs) to social media. The goal is for people to come over to Amazon and watch both. You can make a list of videos you want to be related to and schedule the URLs to auto-post to social media on a regular basis: once a week, month, or quarter.

Besides sharing, you can also indicate a relationship to Amazon through your title and keywords. Browse the detail pages that you wish to connect to. Look at the keywords used in bullets or descriptions, and revise your listing to include these.

Connecting with product pages will be more difficult, if Amazon even allows it at all. It's too early to tell. But theoretically, the more similar your video is to another product, the more likely it will be that Amazon might display your video as a related item.

Even if you are unsuccessful in making your item appear on related product pages, it's a good idea to take a look at these listings. Look for high ranking, best selling, related products. This means products with lots of reviews and a low Best Seller Rank (BSR). The BSR is found in the Product Details area on a product page. The lower this number the better the product is selling.

The next image shows a book BSR. It ranks #942,163 out of all books on Amazon, and it also ranks #76, #126, and #527 compared to other books in specific subcategories.

Amazon Best Sellers Rank: #942,163 in Books (See Top 100 in Books)
#76 in Books > Business & Money > Personal Finance > **College & Education Costs**
#126 in Books > Education & Teaching > Higher & Continuing Education > **Financial Aid**
#527 in Books > Education & Teaching > Schools & Teaching > **Funding**

The subcategories themselves are words that you might use as keywords. You can click through each subcategory to see the type of items within and the words they use in their listings. You would choose the best ones to add to your video.

If you have a product on Amazon, there is a feature where it might be shown as *Related Items* to the right of your video (see the books in the next image). However, this is not yet available to AVD users, but a feature to hope and watch for with new updates.

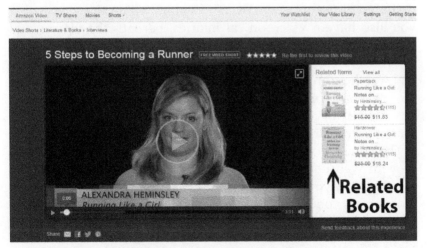

http://www.amazon.com/dp/B00L1I83RW/

Call to Watch the Next Video

You might consider directing people from one video to another. You can use the audio to remind viewers of earlier videos. Simply state at the end, "Look for our follow up video titled... " or "If you missed our previous video titled... " and state that these videos are also found on Amazon.

Multiple Videos with Similar Keywords

It's a good idea to create multiple videos with similar keyword variations. This can help portray you as an authority on a subject, and this should help improve your rankings.

If you made three videos: New York travel, New York trip, and New York vacation, you are beginning to set your brand as an expert on visiting New York.

Customer Keyword Search — Ranks You Higher

Search result positions seem to be significantly impacted by the actions of Amazon customers. If you can get someone to enter certain keywords, search for your video, and then watch it, Amazon deems you highly relevant for those keywords.

This strategy can be used in your video creation. For example, if you end your video on "Cat's Health" telling the viewer that you also have a video on cat injuries, perhaps the viewer will keystroke "cat injury video" into the Amazon search box to look for your video. When this user finds your next video, clicks it, and watches through to the end, this makes your cat injury video more *relevant* for the search term of "cat injury video." Amazon has learned by the user's actions that you are relevant for the search term "cat injury."

The same process could work on a website. If you have an article on your website that ends with, "To find our video on Amazon, just type [say your keyword phrase here] into the search box and look for our company brand" or "Watch our tutorial on Amazon by searching for [say your keywords here]."

Checklist of Ideas to Increase Your Views

1. *Key Art:* Have a great image to entice users to click.

2. *Website Ads:* Add images to your website sidebar with "Watch our videos," or "Free training videos," or "See our product review video."

3. *Audio in Your Video:* End your video with a statement like: "This was a follow-up to our video on (title) which is also found on Amazon.com" or "Look for our other video, (title) also found on Amazon.com."

4. *Short Videos:* Create fast, short videos which encourage viewers to hit pause, rewind, and/or watch again.

5. *Social Media:* Use software to schedule video posts to run quarterly and/or consider running social media ads.

6. *E-mail Newsletters:* Add your video to your newsletter with an announcement that your video is now live and use an image with a link to your video on Amazon.

7. *E-mail Closures:* End your e-mails with something like, "In case you missed it, click here to see our video" or add a link to your signature byline.

8. *E-mail Auto-responders:* Use your e-mail platform to send a link to your video at one point in your funnel path, or have subscribers filter through all your videos over a certain time period.

9. *Thank You Pages:* Add a video link to every landing page, such as the page a user lands on after making a purchase or subscribing to your list. Include the link in your e-mails too.

10. *Ask for Shares:* Ask viewers to share your video.

11. *Joint Ventures:* Offer something extra for leaders and experts in your niche to share your video.

Episodic Videos

As you begin to think about the marketing power of creating videos and how grouping them might help build your credibility and authority, it's time to consider Episodic videos.

The steps are very similar to those used to create a Standalone video. Episodic videos are a series of videos grouped together as a Season. Amazon describes Episodic videos as:

> **"Episodic**
>
> A title (series) consisting of multiple episodes that comprise a season. For example, a TV show ("Transparent") or multi-part documentary. A title can have multiple seasons. For episodic titles available for purchase, you choose if an entire collection (season) or individual videos (episodes) is available for purchase.
>
> . **Series:** The parent title of episodic content. There might be different series for different versions of a show. This is relevant only if it is required to separate the episodic titles into different collections. Example: "Southern Fly Fishing Classic" & "Southern Fly Fishing." Traditionally, all seasons and episodes of a show have a single parent title (series).
>
> **Season:** A collection of individual titles presented in a sequence with other seasons. For shows that are "non-episodic," we suggest collecting under a "season," by broadcast year or production cycle. Example: "Daily Farm Report."
>
> **Episode:** An individual title that is in a sequence with other episodes."

The easiest way to think about these terms is to compare them with a TV show. The *Series* is the title of the show. The *Season* would refer to the first season it was shown on TV, for example Fall 2015. Next, within the season, you have a series of *Episodes*, such as one through twenty, perhaps aired every Wednesday.

Episodic Series are created under the Episodic Tab. The image below shows a Series called "My Test Series." It's already set up and it contains two Seasons.

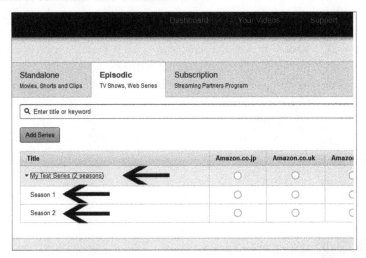

For the purpose of this book tutorial, the first Season was titled "Season 1" and the second was titled "Season 2," but you can name these whatever you like when you set up your Series.

If you click on a Season, it expands and you see the Episodes inside. In the next image, you can see the Series name "My Test Series," and that you are viewing Season 1 (indicated next to the Series Title), and Season 1 contains 2 Episodes, titled "My Episode 1" and "My Episode 2."

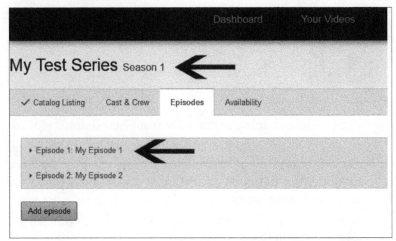

Now that you see the layout structure, you can prepare your own outline for videos you plan to make. This will work for films that tell stories, TV shows, or tutorial courses and classes.

Just because you have a group of videos does not mean that they will perform best as a Season. It's important to understand how Episodic videos appear in Amazon search results so you can make the best decision, based on your business goals.

Here's an example of Amazon search results that show listings for the Game of Thrones Series:

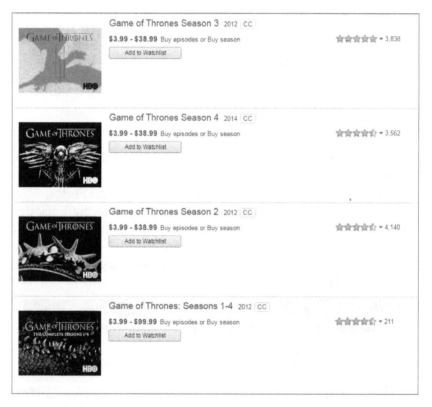

Episodic videos display differently from Standalone videos:

- *Seasons Rank:* The first three listings show that Seasons rank. Customers can still click through and buy a separate Episode, but the Episode itself is not ranking. Episodes do not take up real estate space on a Search Results page.

- *Series Rank:* The bottom listing shows that your Series will appear in Search Results.

It is important to understand that both the Seasons and the Series rank, but not each Episode page. You might consider this when planning your videos. If you have a 12 video course where each video accomplishes a goal of its own and could indeed be watched alone, listing them as Standalone videos, might give you more exposure. You could have 12 items on a search results page. Listing as a Season within a Series, will give you only two listings.

One method is not necessarily better than the other. While it sounds exciting to have your 12 videos conceivably fill every entry on page one for a search term, there is also power in using Seasons. If your 12 videos are listed as a Season, every review gives that Season authority. If a user reviews Episode 1 and 8, your Season will show 2 reviews and have a ranking boost for the 2 reviews. With 12 Standalone videos, there is no Season at all, just two videos with an authority of 1 review (plus 10 videos with no review authority points). This is something positive about Episodic videos: that reviews have more power as a Season since they are grouped together.

If a user clicks on a Season, the landing page that comes up shows the Season with a list of all Episodes that follow. When compared to a Standalone listing, you'll notice that Episodes do not have the *Starring* and *Director* links. If these links are important to your optimization and conversion plan, this might be a reason to NOT choose Episodic videos.

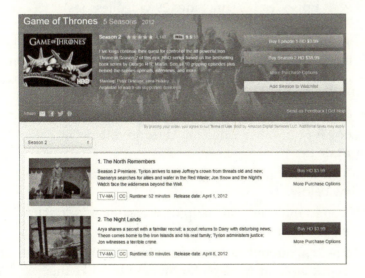

Also, your Episode settings do not have locations for Key Art, so AVD users do not yet have the same features shown in the second Game of Thrones example image, where each Episode has a unique image. Hopefully, this feature will be offered to AVD users in the future.

Although you have some extra steps, the Episodic set up steps are very similar to the Standalone options. One small difference is in your Series Key Art. The first image in the Catalog Listing still uses the horizontal landscape format at a ratio of 16:9 and 1920x1080 pixels, but the second image is also landscape, and uses a ratio of 4:3 and 1600x1200 pixels. This is different from the second Standalone image setting.

Using the Episodic feature will most likely be popular with independent filmmakers creating a film series and tutorial type videos. Courses could be set up as different seasons, all falling under the same Series. Here's an outline example one might write to plan for this concept:

Series Name: Jane's Math Course
    Season 1: Algebra
        Episodes 1-35 (includes 35 video lessons)
    Season 2: Geometry
        Episodes 1-20 (includes 20 video lessons)
    Season 3: Calculus
        Episodes 1-29 (includes 29 video lessons)

Based on their interests and needs, Amazon viewers could purchase the entire math course Series, purchase a chosen Season, or take a look at each Season and purchase individual Episodes.

Some things you *might* be able to use at the very end of your video (so as not to interrupt the viewer experience) are:

- Look for our other video on Amazon called: "mention your title here."

- If you would rate this video five stars, please leave a review below.

- If you found this video helpful, please click below to share it on your favorite social media site.

- To hear about our future videos, bookmark this page and check back on Amazon for more videos like this.

Create Videos that Convert

Sell the Change

Your video message should always be a promise of change. This is the most important factor to make a conversion. What will change for the viewer by watching? If your video is for rent or purchase, the customer envisions something getting better as a result of the purchase, even if the gain is only a change in the viewer's mood, a change of entertainment.

You must rank to have successful *Calls to Action,* but even if you rank, the final conversion comes from the click through. This means you need to have good Key Art and a good synopsis that portrays what will change.

Visitors search for features, but they really want benefits. Try to sell the benefits. A visitor searches for "bike with thick tires," but what he or she *really wants* is change, a solution to flat tires when biking on dirt roads. A video title or synopsis message of, "Enjoy Your Bike on Any Terrain" might convert better than "Our Review of 24×3" Super Balloon Bike Tires."

If you can sell the change and tap into the emotion behind your product or service, your conversions should increase.

Amazon Search Results

To rank your videos in Amazon Search results, you need to be relevant. When a customer enters words into the Amazon Search Box, the immediate results shown are for "All Departments." The customer must choose a *drop-down filter* to search by department, such as only in Electronics or only in Video. Many users do not take time to use the filter. They only add it after the first results are undesirable. This means you need to optimize your listing to compete with all products on Amazon.

When you make changes to your listing, allow two to four weeks to pass before evaluating the impact of your changes. It can take this long for Amazon to fully index and learn what your listing is about and what it is relevant for.

Your Target Audience

Too often, companies begin with video creation and then ask, "How can I rank my video?" As explained thus far, the best path to converting a targeted audience is to establish goals, identify customers and what they search for, and *create video content that matches the customer's keyword search terms.*

Refreshing some essential business marketing concepts should help you rank and run successful video marketing campaigns. You need to have a clear picture of your business objectives, who your customer is, what they are looking for, and how you propose to *solve their problem.* If the wrong person is watching your video, then the video will not be a *path* to increased conversions.

To connect with your buyer, keep the stages of your sales funnel in mind and the value of marketing benefits, rather than features. What is your customer thinking? What does your customer need?

Most business funnels include four phases:

Awareness = What?
Heard of the Product or Service

Interested = Why?
Curious to Learn More

Desire = How?
What's Involved

Take Action
Share
Buy

1. *Awareness:* The top of the funnel represents your general audience. These people are aware you exist. They've heard of your product or service or were just exposed to it through your Amazon video.

2. *Interested:* This is a slightly smaller group of people who have already heard about you and are interested or curious to know why your product or service might be important. They want to watch your video.

3. *Desire:* These people understand your product or service is important and want to know how to get it.

4. *Action:* These people are so excited about your product or service, that they share the information or buy now.

Your most expensive customer is in the *Awareness* phase at the top of the funnel. It will take you time to reach these people and educate them about your product or service. Time really does equate to money when you think about whether you want to spend ten minutes with a customer or ten hours if the result will be the same monetary profit. Your customer in the *Awareness* phase costs you more.

The amount of video shares you receive on social networks can help bring customers into this level. Hopefully every time someone shares your video, the top of your funnel becomes wider. The challenge becomes how to efficiently handle these people within the Amazon platform and terms of service. What will you place in your video content to connect with the viewer?

Amazon reviews can help with the people hanging out in the *Interested* phase. These people want to see what other people said. They will expand the reviews and scroll down to read the entire page before they watch, rent, or buy. Reviews help move them into the *How* and *Buy* phases.

Viewers in the *How* phase are your cautious top of the fence or teeter-totter customers. They may be skeptical. Just one small detail might cause them to click away. They're the ones who say, "I was going to purchase until..." and fill in the blank with the price, poor review, or other excuse. These visitors have their bathing suits on, ready to jump into the pool. You have to make sure the water temperature doesn't scare them away.

Your easiest conversion occurs by connecting to people in the *Take Action* phase. These people may have even purchased a similar solution elsewhere and it failed. Now, they are looking for a better solution. These people are your best Return On Investment, the highest profit received for time and effort you expend.

You don't necessarily have to bring people through each stage of the funnel, but you should know which stage of the funnel each of your videos is targeting. For each stage, your message needs to say or portray why you are the best, trustworthy, and final, valuable solution for the issue at hand.

Circumstances Trump Demographics

You might separate your buying audiences into your funnel categories. For a weight loss business, the person who has tried weight loss programs would fall into the "Buy Now" category of the funnel. However, actors could be an audience too. They are in the awareness category. Actors are aware there are weight loss programs, but they may not be curious until they are assigned a role requiring them to drop ten pounds. Actors may not meet the demographic traits of your typical customer, but circumstances can jump them directly to the "Buy Now" phase. Circumstances *always* trump demographics.

How Long Should My Video Be?

Duration was covered earlier from the viewpoint of ranking your video in Amazon search results, but it also plays a role in conversions. Does your buying audience prefer short or long videos? It does you no good to rank number one for long videos, if your target audience prefers short.

Another strategy is to make fast paced videos. This works well with instructional videos. Don't go so fast that the user leaves, but just fast enough so the user might want to rewind and replay, or even better, watch the entire video over again (and you gain another view).

On fast paced videos, you might remind the visitor in the audio that they can hit the pause button to freeze the screen at any moment. Tell them, "Hit pause to take notes."

While short videos tend to be more desirable, don't forget that a user seeking information will usually sit through *any length* of video as long as it continues to provide value all the way through. You might browse Amazon's longer videos that have significant numbers of reviews and try to determine how they maintain a viewer's attention. Copy their strategies.

How long should my video be? The answer is: as long as it takes to convey your valuable message, and not a second longer.

How Much Free Information?

The biggest concern many business owners have is, "I don't want to give away too much for free." This is often heard from those selling a course or a reference book. The same answer expressed by many video experts is, "Do not to worry about giving away too much for free in your videos."

Focus on your target audience. Some people will only come for the free information. Accept this and realize that these people *never were and will never be* your target audience. Your ideal customer is not the one with the mind-set of, "I can do this myself without purchasing."

If you sold apples, and a visitor arrived looking for pears and walked away, you would not feel bad. It may help to view your "freebie" viewers in this manner. Don't worry that they came, watched, and left. At most, they are considered your top funnel customers, if you can even declare them in your funnel at all. They were never interested in buying what you are selling. Let them go.

If you're fortunate, this freebie audience will still mention your business or share your video. "Hey, I saw this video on Amazon the other day" or "You know you can learn that for free over on Amazon." After all, who wouldn't tell their friends about this great free information your video just provided? This can result in some untraceable word-of-mouth marketing for you.

Train yourself toward a new way of thinking. Ask, "What can I give away for free today, that will bring in future sales?"

Giving valuable free information ultimately builds your trust and credibility. When you present this information, try to include a clever way (within Amazon terms of service) to state a reason to also own the product, become a member, or purchase your service. Let the viewer think, "I needed it for reference" or "I knew I would receive additional quality information with a membership." This will be tricky with Amazon Video Direct because of their terms of service, but it's time to think outside the box. Keep an eye out for other new marketers too. Look for new ideas and copy their example.

Checklist of Questions to Identify a Target Audience

Knowledge Level

1. What problem is this customer trying to solve?

2. What type of knowledge does your viewer already have?

3. Is your brand targeting multi-levels of viewers with different expertise, backgrounds, or goals?

4. Does your audience prefer a short series of tutorials or will they sit through an hour presentation?

5. What does your viewer look for in a successful presentation?

Demographics

6. What is the age, gender, and location of this person?

7. At what time frame of their life is this person trying to solve this issue? (Graduation, divorce, new baby, etc.)

8. What types of issues does your viewer connect with on an emotional level?

9. How does your audience find new videos? (Search Google, browse social media, read e-mails, etc.)

10. What type of video and in what category does your audience watch?

11. What words might this viewer need to hear to pursue an idea or complete your *Call to Action*?

12. At what time of day and where will your audience watch the video? Are they alone or surrounded by co-workers or family members?

Social Interactions

13. What words should your viewer hear to inspire them to share or write a review?

14. What types of videos does your audience share or write reviews on?

15. Where might your audience share your video and are their extended connections interested in your niche?

16. Who are the people your audience follows, comments on, or subscribes to on social networks? Which social site has the greatest amount of your target audience?

Secondary Audience

17. Do you have a secondary audience, with a complimentary interest, who might help convert, persuade, defend, share, or talk about you to your primary audience?

18. Can you find and connect with new contacts and influencers (people with large numbers of followers) by researching trends on social media networks?

19. Who is leaving video reviews on Amazon? Who is commenting on videos on social networks? Can you interact with these people?

20. Can you connect with other content creators? What LinkedIn, Facebook, or Google+ groups might you join?

Price Below the True Value

Psychology plays a role in making a sale. A purchase takes place when the customer perceives the exchange to be in their favor. In basic bartering, there is a swap of goods, and the psychology behind this exchange is that both parties valued the other item more than the item they own. Makes sense.

For paid videos, you want the viewer to feel that what they will receive is worth more than the money paid to Amazon. Your video synopsis must demonstrate the value gained, so the viewer feels the desire to click through.

Are you trustworthy? Why should the viewer purchase from you? What makes you a credible authority on this subject?

As your company creates more videos, your company name or your own name (if you are your brand) will gain exposure. You can build trust with the "been there, done that" approach. You might share your perspective, personal journey, or experience, and tell how your product or service was the solution.

If you intend to charge for videos, you might first begin with some free videos. Teach something today. Teach your best thing, *for free* and viewers are more likely to trust and believe that your future product will be just as compelling. Let customers imagine that if this is the content you give away for free, and it's fantastic, then there must be even more value in your paid video!

Try to have every video provide outstanding content. You want to leave the viewer more educated than they were before they watched.

The fundamentals required to make a conversion never change. Your customer goes through these psychological steps:

- Perceives the item (the video) as valuable,
- Trusts you to be a credible business,
- Has a need that the item will fulfill, and
- Perceives the value of this item to be greater than the cash exchanged for it

If anything fails along this sequence, the customer will stop watching and leave your path to conversion. Your video must bring the customer through the emotional stages above. Video is playing a role in your traffic path to a sales conversion.

Analytics - Your Dashboard

Conversions are more important to rank than any factor previously mentioned. It's discussed last because to convert, you must be found, so it was necessary to research and build your keywords first. The more conversions you have, the higher you rank. If something is converting well, it's popular, so Amazon will show it even more, which results in even more conversions.

Amazon's video dashboard does not yet provide much information concerning conversions. Your dashboard shows minutes viewed and your total earnings. This information can be filtered down by each individual video and location (viewers in the U.S., U.K., Canada, etc.).

There is little to compare when observing competitor videos, except for reviews. You can see if your competitor has more reviews than you, which may or may not mean the video has had more views. Not everyone leaves a review. On the contrary, a platform like YouTube shows the number of views to the public which gives valuable marketing information.

At the moment, your dashboard is a "feel good" or "feel bad" dashboard, because there is not much action you can take from looking at it. You either feel good because you have many views, or you feel bad because you don't.

The number of times your image was shown is referred to as *Impressions*. It would be extremely helpful to know that your Key Art appeared to 1,000 customers and only two clicked through. This would tell you to consider changing your Key Art to fix this poor *click-through rate*. The click through rate is the rate at which people see your image and decide to click through and watch. You want this to be high. However, at the time of this writing, there is no report to show how many people saw your Key Art image in search results, nor how many of these people actually clicked through.

Your dashboard might be useful if you decide to run an outside advertising campaign. You might be able to correlate campaign performance results if you created an e-mail campaign or posted links to social media and the very next day saw a huge jump in views. This is one way you might use your limited dashboard to plan and track some marketing actions.

The best marketing comes from things you can track and thus repeat. This is difficult with the current analytics provided.

Amazon PPC and Video Ads

Amazon has no advertising options as of yet. Ads can help sellers learn more about the needs and actions of a target audience. Amazon does offer advertising in other programs, so this might be added in the future. You should watch for updates.

You might first see Pay Per Click (PPC) ads. These are ads you would create using your Key Art and choice of keywords and they would appear to targeted customers in the search results. You'd pay a fee for each customer click and you'd receive analytic reports on your ad performance.

Another option that might open up is pre-roll ads. In this case you would create a video ad that would appear in front of other Amazon videos. This would be similar to the ads Amazon runs now in front of your own video, except in this case, you would be able to run *your* ad in front of another person's video to give exposure to your brand, product, course, or film. Google offers this and this would be a nice feature for Amazon to add to their program.

Amazon URL Links

The shortest link to your video on Amazon.com, the USA site, will be in a format like this:

https://www.amazon.com/dp/ASIN/

Example:

https://www.amazon.com/dp/B01G2IMWQS/

The shortest link to your video on a non-US site, for example Amazon.co.uk, will include some title words between the site and /dp/ in a format like this:

https://www.amazon.com/Your-Title/dp/ASIN/

Example:

https://www.amazon.co.uk/How-You-Maximize-Student/dp/B01FYR72EU/

When you think about social media marketing, consider sharing URLs to different Amazon locations.

Social Media Networks

What's Shareable?

It's time to take a look at all the social media possibilities we've casually mentioned. Sharing your Amazon video URL to social media networks has the potential to bring in more views, which is good for Amazon search result rankings.

Amazon has sharing icons for e-mail, Facebook, Twitter, and Pinterest on the lower left below your video. You can use these yourself. Simply click on them to share.

It's too early to tell, but perhaps Amazon will approve a video that includes audio at the end that asks, "Please share this video with your friends on social networks." Since Amazon has the social icons, we would think this audio would be accepted. As more people upload videos, groups and forums are the best place to learn about users' experience with Amazon terms.

Sharing can quickly increase views. Sharing goes beyond social media. It takes place any time someone says, "Look at this" which can happen surrounding a TV, at a home computer, in a classroom, in an office setting, and even on a phone.

Anticipate why your audience will share a video. Is it funny, creative, unique, sentimental, or emotional? Is there anything unexpected? What type of video does your audience share and can you make videos like that? How many times have you shared a video on a social network? What was it about the video or audience that made you want to share? As you make your "share requirements" list, check your own videos to see if they meet your criteria. The goal is to create videos people want to share.

Keep in mind that sharing your own videos can impact other statistics, such as the number of "opens" and "click-throughs" from your e-mail campaigns and/or blog subscribers. If these people have already seen your video, they've no reason to click through your e-mail to watch it again on Amazon.

The Amazon Video Direct dashboard is very simple, so stagger your social media postings so you can track which platform brought you the most views.

Schedule Posts on Facebook

You can use Facebook's schedule posting feature to schedule your video once a quarter over the next year. You might post with the opening, "Have you already seen my video on...[topic]."

This scheduling will allow you to pick up some new views from people who became fans after your initial posting. To schedule a Facebook post, paste in your Amazon URL, and click the Publish dropdown menu.

This opens a popup box where you can choose the date and time you want your post to appear. Repeat for each quarter.

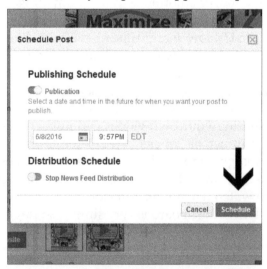

Facebook Ads

Facebook ads are another strategy to increase views. The ads can be targeted toward a specific demographic audience. You can even target fans or followers of your competitor. Use *Fan Page Promoted Posts* to place your ad in front of friends-of-friends or people who liked a competitors Facebook Page. If they like your competitor, they may like your video too.

Look for groups, pages, and influencers who have expertise in video. Try to connect and do some joint ventures with them.

Pinterest

You can create a Pinterest account with a Board for all your videos. Title the Board with your main topic and the word "video." As you create more videos, create new boards grouped by topic. Re-pin your videos to boards that have a mix of items. Occasionally, re-pin the original pin to the same or an new board to give your original pin a refreshing boost. If you original pin has no likes or pins, consider deleting it.

Each of your Pin descriptions on Pinterest should include:

- An enticing title and description with keywords
- The keyword "video" to help your be found well, and
- The Amazon target URL

Auto-posting Amazon Pages to Social Media

To save time, you might use an auto-posting software to schedule your posts to social media sites. When you schedule posts, use all the URL variations of your Amazon listings: the Standalone video, Episode, Season, Series, Starring, Director, and Writer.

Consider using a variety of different images that lead to all variations of your listings on Amazon. For example, you might have five different images that post once a month, but all lead to the same video. This strategy gives the appearance to viewers that you are posting different content, although they all lead to the same destination. There are several software options available. See our favorite and auto-posting tutorials on our website at:
https://www.KidsandMoneyToday.com.

Extend the Reach of Your Videos

Let's face it. Videos take a lot of time to create, or if you have someone create it for you, it's expensive — because videos take a lot of time to create! In the interest of getting the best Return on Investment (ROI), you want to consider re-purposing your video content. This means using the same, rephrased, or slightly altered format of your video to either expand your branding or bring in new audiences.

Checklist for Re-purposing Your Videos

Consider if you can also use your video as a:

1. *Social Connection:* Post the link to social media networks

2. *Podcast:* Extract the audio from a video, upload it to iTunes, and allow people to subscribe to your podcast

3. *PDF:* Convert the audio transcript into a PDF to post on the Internet or maybe the user receives the PDF after signing up on your list

4. *Article:* Turn the PDF into an article for a magazine

5. *Joint Venture Reviews:* Turn the PDF into a spin-off review article, that another company would share to social media or post on their website

6. *CDs and DVDs:* Sell as a CD or DVD or Udemy course; possibly as a training program or a collection set for a niche audience

7. *Webinar:* Hold a webinar to show the video in segments while you explain the topic further or answer questions

8. *Thank-you Note:* Use a video as a free bonus in a thank you e-mail to your customer

Don't worry too much about having your video information in more than one location. In many cases, the person who listens to you on a podcast will not also be following you on Pinterest, Facebook, and other social media networks.

Send More Traffic to Amazon

Rank Your Amazon Video in Google

Besides ranking on Amazon, it would be nice to rank on Google for the same keywords. It's not a secret. The simple rule to ranking on Google is to be relevant. Everything we've addressed thus far contributes to the relevancy of your video. You have tips to:

- Research Keywords
- Create *Calls to Action* related to your topic
- Know the need your target audience searches for
- Share to social networks

All of these play an indirect role in establishing your expertise, authority, and relevancy which will improve your ranking in both Amazon and Google search results for your targeted customer, the one ready to watch your video or film.

Amazon doesn't explain everything that's done with a caption file. Perhaps the coding in the settings of a video listing can also be picked up by Google and thus, captions may help your video be found in Google search results, so be sure to include keywords in your audio that will show up in captions.

Inbound Links to Your Amazon Pages (Backlinks)

Inbound links are one factor Google uses to indicate relevancy. You want links to all URLs associated with your video (Stand-alone, Starring, Writer, Episode, Season, Series and foreign sites like Amazon.co.uk). To create inbound links, promote these URLs as an outbound link on your own website and any joint venture website. Also include these links in your social media shares.

You can manually monitor how your Amazon videos rank in search by creating a spreadsheet and recording the date and ranking position. There are also several types of software to keep track of this. You might try Market Samurai found at:
https://www.kidsandmoneytoday.com/marketsamurai

Trends

When you have had your videos live for a period of time, especially after a year, you can begin to look for trends. Are there peaks and valleys that can be narrowed down to specific days of the week, months, holidays, or promotions you ran? Evaluate what caused the peaks and valleys, make changes with predictions, and reevaluate.

Also keep an eye out for daily trends. What's popular on TV and YouTube, or at the mall, library, or fairs? Try to capitalize on these if they ever relate to your live videos. Remember that you can always update a video!

Affiliate Marketer Links

You can sign up for Amazon's Associate (affiliate) program which allows you to add a small tracking code to all links you post sending customers to Amazon. If these customers make a purchase after clicking your link, whether it is to pay to watch a video or buying another product within 24 hours of clicking, you will receive a small commission for helping create the sale. This is affiliate marketing.

You can also re-purpose any product video you might make for Amazon. Recall that if you have a product on Amazon, you might upload a review video to Amazon with the goal of having the viewer watch and then search for and purchase your product on Amazon. Don't let your video marking efforts stop there. Next, take this same video and upload it to other sites like YouTube and Facebook with an Amazon affiliate link in the description. This link will take the viewer over to Amazon and you will receive a commission for any purchase made within 24 hours.

Finally, you can take the YouTube embed coding and add it to your blog or website, again using an Amazon affiliate link to your product. Again, you'll get credit for any sales made within 24 hours of clicking this link.

The Amazon Associate commissions are fairly small, but since you are creating inbound links anyway, they may as well be coded with an affiliate tag to generate some extra income. Pennies can add up!

A Repeatable Video System

Here's a quick summary of concepts we've covered so far. For a successful *Video Marketing Plan*, you should know:

- What you want your visitor to do,
- What keywords they use to look for solutions,
- What your targeted customer wants emotionally,
- What your plan is to rank well,
- Where you will post your video for exposure,
- How you will measure the success of each video

A *Video Marketing Plan* is different from a *Repeatable Video System*. The plan is about marketing. The system is about your production process. You want to have an efficient, repeatable system. As your income grows, you might entertain the idea of outsourcing certain aspects of this process.

A good strategy for creating videos is to produce groups of videos together. This has been referred to as batch processing or segment processing. You have to decide what is better: batch processing or one-by-one video completion?

In a factory, you see ten people completing a task in an assembly line, but each person is actually doing the same task again and again. Each person is batch or segment processing.

The presumption is segment processing (completing several instances of a task) is most efficient. You could break apart the main tasks for video. These are: idea, script, film, edit, upload, and promote. To segment or batch process, you begin by setting a time to write all your video ideas, the focus, the *Call to Action,* and how you will measure the video's success.

In the next segment, you'd write the script for each video idea. Next, you would set a time to film all your videos. (If you do this, change your clothes between takes or wear branded clothing, so when you upload your videos, it will look as though each video was filmed on a different day.)

During the filming, prioritize your schedule by beginning with the least important video. As you film, the audio, techniques, and how natural your voice sounds will all improve, and as a result, your final, most important video will have the highest quality.

In the editing segment, you might link videos together and possibly reuse clips across videos, such as introductions or exit frames. The final segment of your video system would be to upload, schedule, optimize, and share the video.

The benefit of a segment processing approach is that you can eventually outsource a segment. You can hire someone to do all the editing, while you focus on filming.

Outsourcing may be a difficult decision if you love all parts of the creation process. Maybe you enjoy trying different audio, want to experiment with lighting, and so on. But to really grow a business, you usually need to transition out of the creation process and learn to delegate.

Batch processing videos works very well, but this should only be done *after* you have completed your first few videos and only accomplished in *small batches*.

The benefits of completing one full video at a time, one-by-one videos, are actually *more efficient* for *business growth*. This is because you:

- Don't waste time changing your train of thought from the message of one video to the next.
- Find and learn from mistakes early.
  - You don't want to be editing 20 videos and then, discover a recording issue. Especially with AVD, there are so many possible errors in the approval process, that you will learn a lot by beginning with a single video completions.
- Gain the psychological satisfaction and motivation from finishing a job through to completion.
- Go live sooner which increases self accomplishment, starts your royalty revenue faster, and may motivate you to create more.

Plan Your Videos

Completion, Quality, and Quantity

Videos and films are really never finished. Videos are like writing or designing websites, the piece can almost always be improved. At some point, you will have to decide what is "good enough" or "a good start" for the action you wish to accomplish and make the decision to upload and go live. Your business objective is targeted traffic, exposure, or conversions, but not the perfect video.

With every video or book or seminar (if you attend them), you will learn something new, and it's important to allow yourself to learn as you grow. Completion *always* trumps quality and quantity. Completion brings conversions.

This doesn't mean you should upload low quality or boring videos of no value. Quality will impact your ranking, and you want to be found. Instead, this means to accept the fact that your videos will not be perfect and will always have room to improve. On Amazon, since you can always upload a new, updated version, there's no reason to wait around for perfection.

Prioritize

Every business decision should be made thinking about:

1. Profitability and/or exposure (if you goal is not monetary),

2. Ease of implementation, and

3. Repetitiveness

Emotion is not on this list. You might use a spreadsheet to create a video-to-do list as a means to rank and prioritize your video ideas. This will help keep your decision making analytical rather than emotional.

You don't want to create the fun video. Create the one that meets your business goal.

Our sample spreadsheet lists video ideas with corresponding columns for: profit rating, ease of use, and repetitiveness. (Use your own opinion to add ratings from 1 to 10.) Sum these values across and work on the video with the highest value first.

Sample spreadsheet:

Video Idea	Profit	Ease	Repeatable	Value (sum)
A	5	2	10	17
B	9	9	1	19
C	2	9	9	20

Your *Profit* value might show 5 for a 50 percent profit, 9 would be 90 percent, and so on.

The *Ease* column represents how easy it is to make the video. If your video involves another person, it is more difficult. It is even more difficult should you have to film from the air, which might mean you will have the expense of hiring a pilot or someone who films with a drone.

Repeatable means either the video produces consistent monthly cash, or the system itself is repeatable (such as a template video where you can easily create more videos by simply changing a slide or clip). You could even separate these two thoughts into two unique columns.

You might even want to create additional columns with factors to incorporate your own value ideas.

Sum across and you see that in the spreadsheet above, video C, which actually ranks as the least profitable, would be worked on first. It is easy to make and is in some manner, repeatable. Sometimes, consistent fast cash can be a higher priority than a large one time profit that will occur at some date in the future.

Get Creative

You can add variety to your videos by changing the setting. Try indoors, outdoors, a flat background, long hallway, or green screen. Change your clothes and music, or include production bloopers. Try using black and white footage. Film into a mirror or out in the rain. Purchase a special effect clip. Use animation. You might browse photography magazines to obtain inspiration.

Checklist of Ideas for Video Topics, Types, or Themes

A good place to begin creating your video idea list is to use the questions you answered to identify your audience, along with your keyword research. Try these ideas for more inspiration:

Emotion

1. *Motivate:* Make a "You can do this..." video.

2. *Influence Others:* Create a video petition, call to write congress, elect a politician, etc..

3. *Collect Donations:* Do a video for a cause or charity.

Brand Building

4. *Branding:* Create a video establishing your expertise in this field (similar to education videos).

5. *About Page:* Documentary style. Tell how your business was started; include a subtle connection to a product or service for sale.

6. *Promotions, Announcements, and Teasers:* Forecast new product releases, future training videos, or an upcoming contest, event, holiday sale, or special occasion.

Products or Service

7. *Sales Generation and/or Product Features:* Sell your product, service, or affiliate product.

   — Careful with Amazon Terms of Service.

8. *Educate:* Share knowledge, updates, news, documentary ideas, teaching, or training. (Target the audience in the research or learning phase of your sales funnel.)

9. *Information:* Give one tip and send the user to your website to learn more.

   — Careful with Amazon Terms of Service.

10. *Shopping Hauls:* Talk about your purchases and how they relate to your product as you unpack your shopping bag.

11. *Stories:* Tell a story of how someone used your product.

12. *How to*: Create problem solving videos

13. *Comparison Reviews:* Show one product or concept compared to another, and state the pros and cons.

14. *Testimonial or Endorsement Reviews:* Ask others to do a video review of your brand or product.

15. *Demonstration:* Similar to reviews or testimonials, but instead include a visual demonstration of unique, unusual, or funny ways to use your product or service.

16. *Quick Start Guide:* Make a video that's a visual representation of the printed quick start guide a customer might receive with a product purchase.

Customer Interaction

17. *Contest:* Talk about your experience running a contest

18. *Quiz*: Make a video with questions and answers

19. *Increase Traffic:* Make videos where the primary purpose is for the viewer to search for your name or website.

    — Careful with Amazon Terms of Service, you must be subtle here.

20. *List Building or Lead Generation:* Create a video that is so enticing that you expect viewers would Google your brand, land on your page, and sign up for your list.

21. *Add Social Media Exposure:* Create sharable videos

22. *Increase Customer Connection:* Aim to increase reviews by covering trending or controversial topics.

23. *FAQ:* Make a video that answers questions.

24. *Decrease Customer Contact:* Create videos that teach, and as a result, decrease your customer support calls.

Sketch Your Story

Once you have a video idea, its objective, and duration, make a short outline of what you are trying to accomplish. Think about your audience based on backgrounds and needs. Some viewers may already have knowledge on your subject, while others are beginners. When you attempt a video that will reach multiple levels, consider creating an introduction slide to quickly bring everyone up to speed. An opening slide might show the agenda or path to take. Longer videos might show this slide again midway through, to help viewers keep track of the progression of events.

Another approach to keep viewers with expertise interested, is to foreshadow or tease about the subject you will cover.

Your story sketch should be short. You will add more details in the next step, making the script. Sketch a "storyboard." Draw a box for each scene with a short description and *Call to Action*.

Think about how you tell the story. Stories keep the viewer engaged and help make films successful. Stories are made up of problems or conflicts. Viewers can relate to the characters from their own personal experiences or experiences of their family, friends, and clients. Stories conclude with a solution or change (your *Call to Action*).

Your introduction sets the scene. It answers why you are doing the video, what your goal is, and how you will answer the problem. This is where you make an emotional connection with your visitors' needs and opinions.

You might present slides or charts of collected information. Statistics can help explain a solution or provide justification for your position. Keep slides simple and mix the styles. Use charts, bar graphs, and pie charts. Comparison slides are also good.

However, stories are *always* better than diagrams or bar charts illustrating and analyzing statistics. Charts and numbers stimulate the mind, but do nothing for the heart. *Bullet points are bad for viewer retention.* They don't convey a message of entertainment or fun. Think about TV how-to shows—like cooking. How many contain bullet points?

Authentic stories should inspire and persuade without being patronizing. Use emotions to convey energy and excitement and appeal to the heart. Identify some key events that propel your story forward. These might be good locations for *Calls to Action*.

Checklist for Your Story Concept

1. Make a storyboard. Using pen and paper, draw boxes of scene one, two, and so on with a short description of the message portrayed in each scene and what the viewer will see (props, person, etc.).

2. What is the goal of the video? Review your lists of *Calls to Action*. The video needs to tell the viewer what to do, why they should do it, and how they should do it. Visually portray a solution to the problem.

   — Careful with Amazon terms of service.

3. How can you make an emotional connection to increase your conversions? People reach for their wallets when they empathize, feel similar, or relate to the problem at hand. Your video story might share a personal journey, tell how you overcome an obstacle, talk about a lesson learned, or perhaps convey a caution. Can the story connect with personal dreams of success and happiness?

4. Who, if anyone should be in the video? Who connects best with the audience's age, demographics, or interests?

5. If you are in the video, how will you introduce yourself?

6. State the problem or need you are solving. Does your story answer a journalist's questions:

   - Who, what, and when? - Concerning your product
   - Where? - Where is the service or product used?
   - Why? - Why is the price a valuable exchange for the product?
   - How? - How will your story create motivation to buy, search for your company, sign up or accomplish the *Call to Action*.

7. Add your viewpoint. People want to know your thoughts; your opinion. Tell why you endorse or believe in the product, service, or solution.

8. Ask yourself: What will make this video shareable?

Script

After you have your storyboard, make a script. Changes made during scripting can save you hours of editing later. Scripting is also good practice for future outsourcing. If you are used to writing scripts, you will be prepared to eventually hand them to someone, and say, "I need a video for this."

The script is more than dialogue. The script is dialogue plus visual images. You might write dialogue on top of your storyboard or a page of dialogue with notes about visual images. As you write, ask yourself what images might go well with the dialogue. *People come to video because they want to see something,* so you need to give them action on the screen.

Stories are supposed to show and not tell. This is even more true when it comes to video. Look for dialogue that can be replaced with an image. This will also help make your video shorter.

Don't forget about energy. The camera drains your energy. This means you appear less enthusiastic when viewed on a video than when someone talks to you in person. This is why news casters have to smile all the time and make gestures. A video competes with everything else in the room. It's easy for a viewer to look away, so when writing your script, think about how you will keep your video full of energy.

You can observe TV commercials for ideas. Observe how fast the image changes in relation to the audio. Often audio begins before the viewer actually sees the person who's talking. Write down techniques you might use to appeal to your target audience.

Have a great title. Try browsing other videos or book covers for ideas on how to grab a viewer's attention.

Here are specific ideas and strategies for your script language:

- *Keywords:* Use them immediately in the beginning, once or twice in the middle (these might be long-tail versions), and again at the end.
- *About you:* "I'm author, founder, inventor, (etc.) of..."
- *Forecasting:* "I'm going to show you..." "I'm going to explain... but first, I want to ask you, tell you, show you... "
- *Educate:* "Here are some simple (lessons, tips, ...) on..."
- *Authentic:* "Because of my experience in..."

- *Honest:* "While I'm a novice at... I do know about..."
- *Vision:* "My (mission, goal, etc.) is..."
- *Promise:* "This video will show [# of] things you can do today to..."
- *Offer:* "If you [do this] I will personally (send you, give you, tell you, etc.)..."
- *Emotional Connections:* "Have you ever felt...," "Has this ever happened to you?" or "I can't stand it when..."
- *Emotional Change:* "What I learned from... that helped me was... "
- *Convince:* "Some fundamental points about... are..."
- *Sandwich approach:* Tell what you will cover, explain the issue at hand, and then summarize what you just said.

When you have a complete script, let it sit for a day or so. Come back and try to cut the number of words in half. This helps you be as concise as you can, and eliminate any fluff. Viewers want a quality video providing value in as little time as possible.

Read it out loud. Record yourself reading the script. Play it back. Can it stand on it's own, in case you want to turn it into a podcast? Does it sound like you? Is it a conversational, dinner table tone or too sales pitchy?

Read your script pacing back and forth as if you were the head speaker at a conference. Is it natural? Don't hesitate to write "chuckle" or "pause" into your script to make it sound more natural. Include notes for when you should look directly into the camera. Keep this simulated eye-to-eye contact short, just as you would when talking to a friend.

Have someone else read your script and give you feedback.

If you decide to film yourself using a Teleprompter, consider wearing sunglasses—no one will be able to tell you are reading. Ideally, limit your own time on camera in one location to 10-15 seconds, which equates to 2-3 sentences.

Interrupt your speaking with images, slides, white boarding (an animated hand drawing an image), or animation. These type of clicks are often called *B Roll*. You might splice together several clips of you talking so you are first located on screen left and next, on screen right. This change of location diverts the viewers focus and helps maintain interest.

Playing a role may help you relax and sound conversational. Pretend you are a tour bus guide or a teacher in front of a classroom. You are the expert telling them about the solution. Add notes to your script to remind you to use your hands, hold the product, or make some gestures.

Screen Captures

Screen captures are instructional or tutorial videos that show you clicking around a computer screen to complete steps. Follow these script and procedure tips for a clean professional result:

1. Record the entire process with audio, including all the pauses and any mistakes.

2. Take the audio and type it out as a script.

3. Edit the script, cutting out any unnecessary dialogue.

4. Re-record the audio adding natural inflections.

5. Match the audio to the video in your favorite video editing software. You may have to clip the audio into segments or have to speed up portions of the screen capture so everything is aligned properly (in sync).

Audio Presentation Tips

Good audio is the *number one priority* in video creation. If the sound is poor, viewers will click away. Rehearse and record your script twice. The second recording always sounds more natural.

It's easier to match video to previously created audio, so after you have your script, create your audio first. Unless you are filming live, you can create your audio separately. Do this for screen capture, animation, white boarding, or slide presentations.

Download and use the free, user-friendly Audacity software found at: http://audacity.sourceforge.net/.

Checklist for Your Video Presentation

1. *Have energy:* Laugh, smile, and try to imitate mannerisms used on TV. No monotone.

2. *Clap your hands on mistakes:* If you make a mistake recording audio, clap loudly. This sound will help to properly align video with audio during editing.

3. *Use casual conversational audio:* Speak in a tone similar to that you would use talking to a friend over coffee. Better yet, have a friend be there while you film and actually talk to this person.

4. *Talk through the camera:* Talk as if someone is standing behind the camera or 6 feet in front of you. If a friend is helping you film, have them stand behind the camera.

5. *Tease and foreshadow:* Keep the viewer's attention and encourage them to keep watching. Say things like:
   - I'll have an offer for you at the end
   - This is step one of the three I will cover

6. *Add a wake-up call:* Bring drifting viewers back in.
   - Add a surprise prop or have a noise pop in
   - Say, "Remember you can hit pause to see this [chart]"

7. *Keywords:* Use your keywords several times in the audio, so they appear in the caption transcript and help with ranking.

8. *Make a verbal Call to Action:* Add your number one goal or objective to the audio.

9. *Include a social request:* In your audio, ask the viewer to share or leave a review.

10. *Do a "So What?" check:* When you think you are done, ask yourself why the viewer cares about this video and why he or she would share it to a friend?

Editing & Upload

Make interesting videos. Will your video include a person? On what type of background? Do you want to use a green screen to place the person on unique backgrounds? Will you add pop-up items within the video? How will you create your branding message? What music will you choose to set the tone?

To keep viewers attention when someone is talking, pop in an image overlay. This could be an object illustrating the concept (such as question marks for "idea" popping into a tutorial). You might also try an action or special effect illustrating a concept. You can find graphic sources in the back of this book.

You have roughly eight seconds to capture a viewers attention. For most videos, you should open with exactly what you bring to the table. Tell the viewer what they will see today; follow with your five second branding, and begin the information.

An exception is when creating a video ad. For ads, you might open with your branding, because even if the viewer clicks away, they have seen your logo or website URL and heard your *Call to Action*.

Edit out extra breathing, unnatural pauses, and background sound. Was a fire engine passing by?

Close your video with as much visual *Call to Action* as permitted on Amazon. Perhaps show the product or your office, but be careful to not go too far or your video won't be approved.

Use your software to end your video with three boxes in a row with thumbnail images and readable text that show other videos you've uploaded to Amazon. The text might say: Favorite Video, Next Video, or More Amazon videos on this topic. Use an awesome thumbnail image in each box and have the audio say, "look for our other videos on Amazon."

Check for user retention. Does your viewer need to watch to the end to see how it will end? Is it viewable on a small screen like a cell phone? Play your video to someone else for feedback. Watch the video without sound. Listen to the video without viewing the footage. Is it clear? This means it's also podcast ready.

Covered everything? Then, it's time to upload and optimize.

Quick Summary Checklists

Video Marketing Plan

Summary:
- Determine your goals.
- Know your audience.
- Create videos for this audience.
- Rank well for this audience so they will convert.

Detailed:

1. Make a list of your goals and objectives. Include a calendar schedule, such as your plan during holidays.

2. Create your *Calls to Action* to achieve these goals.

3. Identify your target audience and what they want from an emotional perspective.

4. Research the keywords your audience uses to find their solutions.

5. Research niche leaders you might connect with.

6. Understand the stages in your sales funnel.

7. Make a plan to bring viewers to a desired state (buying, writing reviews, buying, searching for you, and so on).

8. Optimize your videos to rank in the top positions for your keywords on search engines and Amazon.

9. Make a prediction for the outcome of each video uploaded.

10. Decide how you will measure the success of each video.

Repeatable Video System

1. Prioritize your video ideas based on analytical data.

2. Apply all the concepts from your *Video Marketing Plan Checklist*: What is the goal, the *Call to Action*, etc.

3. Sketch your story: A storyboard of each scene

4. Write and edit your script. Detailed text along with gestures, *Call to Action* verbiage and images, etc.

5. What makes the video shareable?

6. Audio: Record and edit your audio script to be sure it uses keywords.

7. Film: Create your video footage with a camera or Power Point, animation, or screen capture software. (This might be done together with the audio step, if you plan for a person to talk.)

8. Edit: Finalize your video using your favorite software. Include keywords, a visual, and an audio *Call to Action*.

9. Create Images: Key Art for Amazon Video Direct and any other sizes for blogs and social media posts.

10. Upload your video.

11. Complete all the steps in the *Video Optimization & Marketing* checklist.

12. Monitor your rankings and conversions using software and analytics. Evaluate and adjust as needed.

13. Repeat: Review this checklist again for each video. Batch process in small groups.

Video Optimization & Promotion

1. Create your *Title* and *Synopsis* using keywords.

2. Upload your custom Key Art images.

3. Check that you used keywords in your audio so they are included in your caption file.

4. Choose your Royalty settings.

5. Share to social media directly from Amazon, but also post variations of all the Amazon URLs manually or using a auto-posting software to create inbound links, help with Google ranking, and increase your views.

6. Post variations of Amazon links on your website too.

7. Post your website article URLs containing video links to social media sites and auto-post these links throughout the year. The user may follow this path from social media to your blog to Amazon.

8. Try to connect with influencers in your niche and arrange for them to share links to either your blog post or the Amazon video URL.

9. Re-purpose your video for any of these marketing ideas:
   - Newsletter link
   - Article Reviews
   - Podcasts
   - PDF
   - Sale of a DVD
   - Webinar
   - Google+ Hangout presentation
   - Thank You e-mail confirmation links

10. Consider running an AdWords or Facebook campaign, evaluate it, modify as needed, and run again

Analytics Questions

1. How well are your videos ranking for their primary keyword or phrase on Amazon? On Google Search?

2. How well are your videos ranking for secondary and long-tail keywords?

3. Are you adjusting your titles and descriptions to take advantage of popular topics, holidays, and daily trends?

4. Can you do more to increase your video views?

5. Are you taking a look at competitor videos in the same niche and consider making similar ones and/or taking notes on the keywords they are using?

6. Are you evaluating where your videos are shared?

7. Can you make more videos similar to those that pull in the most income?

8. Have you run any social media campaigns that brought in significant views, and then repeated the process?

9. Sign up for Google Analytics. It's free. After a period of time, review your reports. Can you tell from your Google Analytics which people leave your website to watch your videos on Amazon? Which amazon links are being clicked on your blog?

10. Check Google Analytics for social trends. When you post a video to social media that links to your blog, look in your analytics to see which social network brought the most traffic. Repeat the posts on the social site that performs the best.

Resources

The following resources (free and paid) may assist you with your video marketing strategies. Please read all terms of use.

Apps

- *FiLMmic Pro App:* (Best Video App of 2011)
- iMovie Video Editing App for iPad

Audio

- http://audiojungle.net/
- http://audacity.sourceforge.net/
- http://incompetech.com/
- http://www.premiumbeat.com
- http://www.shockwave-sound.com
- http://triplescoopmusic.com
- http://www.yakitome.com/tts/text_to_speech

Captions

- http://www.3playmedia.com
- http://mediaaccessgroupwgbh.org/
- http://www.nikse.dk/subtitleedit/
- https://www.rev.com
- http://www.subply.com
- http://www.visualdatamedia.com
- http://www.vitac.com

CD & DVD

- http://www.createspace.com/Products/DVD/
- http://www.cdbaby.com/
- http://www.kunaki.com/

Education - Video How To

- http://www.YouTube.com/videomaker
- http://www.videomaker.com/YouTube
- http://www.videomaker.com/magazine/

Graphics

- https://www.canva.com/
- http://cooltext.com/
- http://creativecommons.org/
- http://www.iconfinder.com/
- http://openclipart.org/
- http://www.presentermedia.com/
- http://us.fotolia.com/

Keyword Research Tools

- https://www.google.com/trends/
- http://www.keywordtooldominator.com
- http://keywordtool.io/
- http://www.keywordinspector.com/
- https://www.kidsandmoneytoday.com/marketsamurai
- https://ubersuggest.io/
- http://app.scientificseller.com/keywordtool

Monetizing with Video - Scale Up (Multiple Income Streams)

- http://coull.com/
- https://www.udemy.com/
- https://vimeo.com/
- https://www.youtube.com/

Outsourcing

- http://fiverr.com/
- https://www.upwork.com/
- http://www.taskrabbit.com/

PodCast Help

- http://www.libsyn.com/
- http://www.podbean.com/
- http://www.scribd.com/

Rank Checking

- https://www.kidsandmoneytoday.com/marketsamurai
- https://www.kidsandmoneytoday.com/rank-checker/

Social Media Sharing & Scheduling Your Video URLs

- https://kidsandmoneytoday.com/mass-planner/
- http://ifttt.com/

Teleprompter

- OnAir App from iTunes

Video Creation - Ideas, Tools, and Tips

- http://www.animoto.com
- http://www.flixpress.com/
- http://www.pond5.com/
- http://snapguide.com/
- https://teach.udemy.com/course-creation/hot-topic-courses/
- http://videohive.net/

Video Distribution (Repurposing Your Videos)

- http://www.easywebvideo.com/
- http://www.tubemogul.com/
- http://wistia.com/

Genre Choices - Master List

Action
Action - Comic
Action - Crime
Action - Disaster
Action - Espionage
Action - Future
Action - Hong Kong
Action - Law Enforcement
Action - Martial Arts
Action - Romantic
Action - Superheroes
Action - Sword and Sandal
Action - War
Adventure
Adventure - Comic
Adventure - Romantic
Animation
Animation - Anime
Animation - Cartoons
Animation - Fairy Tales
Animation - Science Fiction
Animation - Sitcom
Art House
Bollywood
Children's Cinema
Children's Television
Children's Video
Children's Video - Educational
Classics
Comedy
Comedy - Animation
Comedy - Dark
Comedy - Family Life
Comedy - Farce
Comedy - Mockumentary
Comedy - Parody
Comedy - Romantic

Comedy - Satire
Comedy - Screwball
Comedy - Sitcom
Comedy - Sketcj
Comedy - Slapstick
Comedy - Sports
Comedy - Stand-up
Drama
Drama - Bilgraphical
Drama - Coming of Age
Drama - Courtroom
Drama - Crime
Drama - Espionage
Drama - Family Life
Drama - Historical
Drama - Medical
Drama - Political
Drama - Religious
Drama - Sports
Drama - Supernatural
Epic
Faith and Spirituality
Faith and Spirituality - Christianity
Faith and Spirituality - Judaism
Faith and Spirituality - Buddhism
Faith and Spirituality - Hinduism
Faith and Spirituality - New Age
Family Cinema
Family Television
Fantasy
Fitness
Fitness - Barre
Fitness - Beginner
Fitness - Cardio
Fitness - Dance
Fitness - Intermediate
Fitness - Interval Training
Fitness - Martial Arts and Boxing
Fitness - Pilates

Fitness - Strength
Fitness - Stretch
Fitness - Yoga
Food and Wine
Food and Wine - Baking
Food and Wine - Barbecuing & Grilling
Food and Wine - Beverages
Food and Wine - Beverages - Beer
Food and Wine - Wine
Food and Wine - Cocktails & Spirits
Food and Wine - Beverages - Coffee & Tea
Food and Wine - Breakfast & Brunch
Food and Wine - Cooking Instruction
Food and Wine - Desserts & Sweets
Food and Wine - Food Stories
Food and Wine - Healthy Cooking
Food and Wine - International
Food and Wine - Lunch & Dinner
Food and Wine - Seasonal Cooking
Food and Wine - Snacks
Food and Wine - Vegetarian and Vegan Cooking
Game Shows
Video Games
Video Games - Action Games
Video Games - Adventure Games
Video Games - Arcade Games
Video Games - Board Games
Video Games - Card Games
Video Games - Children's Games
Video Games - Educational Games
Video Games - Music and Dancing Games
Video Games - Puzzle Games
Video Games - Racing Games
Video Games - Role Playing Games
Video Games - Simulation Games
Video Games - Sports Games
Video Games - Strategy Games
Video Games - Trivia Games
Gay Cinema

Gay Television
Holiday
Horror - Body Horror
Horror - Classic
Horror - Comedy
Horror - Creature Features
Horror - Documentary
Horror - Extreme
Horror - Gothic Horror
Horror - Haunted Houses
Horror - Human Killers
Horror - Monsters
Horror - Paranormal
Horror - Psychological Thrillers
Horror - Slashers
Horror - Supernatural
Horror - Survival Horror
Horror - Teen
Horror - Vampires
Horror - Zombies
Independent - Argentina
International - Australia
International - Balkins
International - Brazil
International - Canada
International - Chile
International - China
International - Cuba
International - Czech Republic
International - Denmark
International - Egypt
International - Finland
International - France
International - Germany
International - Greece
International - Hungary
International - Iceland
International - India
International - Iran

International - Ireland
International - Israel
International - Italian
International - Japan
International - Korea
International - Latin America
International - Mexico
International - Middle East
International - Netherlands
International - New Zealand
International - Norway
International - Peru
International - Philippines
International - Poland
International - Russia
International - Slovakia
International - Taiwan
International - Thailand
International - Turkey
International - United Kingdom
International - United States
International - Vietnam
Lesbian Cinema
Lesbian Television
LGBT
Military
Military - Action
Military - Comic
Military - Dramatic
Mind and Body
Mind and Body - Meditation
Miniseries
Music Concert Footage
Music Video
Music Video - Alternative
Music Video - Blues
Music Video - Christian and Gospel
Music Video - Classic Rock
Music Video - Classical

Music Video - Country
Music Video - Dance & Electronic
Music Video - Folk
Music Video - Hip Hop
Music Video - Jazz
Music Video - Latin
Music Video - Metal
Music Video - New Age
Music Video - Opera
Music Video - Pop
Music Video - Reggae
Music Video - Rock
Music Video - Singer Songwriter
Music Video - Soul
Music Video - World Music
Music Video - Comic
Music Video - Dramatic
Mystery
Mystery - Comic
Mystery - Courtroom
Mystery - Crime
Mystery - Detectives
Mystery - Film Noir
Mystery - Procedural
News Shows
News Shows - Local News
News Shows - World News
Nonfiction
Nonfiction - Architecture
Nonfiction - Automotive
Nonfiction - Award Winners
Nonfiction - Beauty and Fashion
Nonfiction - Beauty and Fashion - Fashion Design
Nonfiction - Beauty and Fashion - Fashion Shows
Nonfiction - Beauty and Fashion - Hair Care
Nonfiction - Beauty and Fashion - Makeup
Nonfiction - Beauty and Fashion - Men's Fashion
Nonfiction - Beauty and Fashion - Perfumes & Fragrances
Nonfiction - Beauty and Fashion - Shopping and Accessorizing

Nonfiction - Beauty and Fashion -Skin Care
Nonfiction - Beauty and Fashion -Wardrobe Advice
Nonfiction - Business and Finance
Nonfiction - Business and Finance - Personal Finance
Nonfiction - Career & Jobs
Nonfiction - Civilization
Nonfiction - Computers
Nonfiction - Computers - Information Technology
Nonfiction - Computers - Networking & Security
Nonfiction - Computers - Programming
Nonfiction - Computers - Software Development
Nonfiction - Computers - Web
Nonfiction - Crafts
Nonfiction - Crime
Nonfiction - Design
Nonfiction - Documentary
Nonfiction - Documentary - Biography
Nonfiction - Educational
Nonfiction - Educational - Early Childhood Education
Nonfiction - Educational - Higher Education
Nonfiction - Educational - Primary & Secondary Education
Nonfiction - Educational - Professional & Career Development
Nonfiction - Educational - Study Aids & Test Prep
Nonfiction - Educational - Teacher's Guides
Nonfiction - Educational - Training & Certification
Nonfiction - Engineering
Nonfiction - Entertainment
Nonfiction - Entertainment - Celebrities
Nonfiction - Entertainment - Movies & Filmmaking
Nonfiction - Entertainment - TV
Nonfiction - Faith and Spirituality
Nonfiction - Games
Nonfiction - Health
Nonfiction - Health - Diets & Weight Loss
Nonfiction - Health - Men's Health
Nonfiction - Health - Mind & Body
Nonfiction - Health - Nutrition
Nonfiction - Health - Personal Health
Nonfiction - Health - Women's Health

Nonfiction - History
Nonfiction - Hobbies
Nonfiction - Holidays
Nonfiction - Home & Garden
Nonfiction - Home & Garden - Gardening
Nonfiction - Home & Garden - Home Buying & Real Estate
Nonfiction - Home & Garden - Pet Care
Nonfiction - Human Spirit
Nonfiction - How To & Instructional
Nonfiction - How To & Instructional - Courses & Lessons
Nonfiction - How To & Instructional - Home Improvement
Nonfiction - Interviews
Nonfiction - Language Instruction
Nonfiction - Law
Nonfiction - Lectures
Nonfiction - LGBT
Nonfiction - Literature
Nonfiction - Mathematics
Nonfiction - Medical
Nonfiction - Military & Way
Nonfiction - Music
Nonfiction - Nature and Wildlife
Nonfiction - Philosophy
Nonfiction - Photography
Nonfiction - Politics
Nonfiction - Psychology
Nonfiction - Relationships
Nonfiction - Science
Nonfiction - Science - Biology
Nonfiction - Science - Chemistry
Nonfiction - Science - Medicine
Nonfiction - Science - Physics
Nonfiction - Science - Science History
Nonfiction - Science - Space Science & Astronomy
Nonfiction - Self-Help
Nonfiction - Social Sciences
Nonfiction - Sports
Nonfiction - Technology
Nonfiction - Transportation

Nonfiction - Travel -
Nonfiction - Travel - Africa
Nonfiction - Travel - Asia
Nonfiction - Travel - Australia & Oceania
Nonfiction - Travel - Central America & Caribbean
Nonfiction - Travel - Europe
Nonfiction - Travel - Middle East
Nonfiction - Travel - South America
Nonfiction - Travel - United States & Canada
Nonfiction - Travel - Beaches
Nonfiction - Travel - Cities
Nonfiction - Travel - Destinations
Nonfiction - Travel - Jungle & Rainforests
Nonfiction - Travel - Mountains & Lakes
Nonfiction - Travel - Small Towns & Rural Areas
Nonfiction - Travel - Tours
Nonfiction - Visual Arts
Nonfiction - Visual Arts - Photography
Nonfiction - Weddings
Performing Arts
Performing Arts - Dance Performance
Performing Arts - Opera Performance
Performing Arts - Classical Music
Performing Arts - Theater
Period Piece
Reality TV
Romantic Comedy
Science Fiction
Science Fiction - Action
Science Fiction - Adventure
Science Fiction - Comic
Science Fiction - Futuristic
Science Fiction - Space Adventure
Sitcoms
Sketch Comedy
Soap Operas
Sports
Sports - Auto Racing
Sports - Baseball

Sports - Basketball
Sports - BMX and Extreme Biking
Sports - Boating and Sailing
Sports - Boxing
Sports - Cycling
Sports - Extreme Sports
Sports - Fishing
Sports - Football
Sports - General Martial Arts
Sports - Golf
Sports - Hunting
Sports - Live Events
Sports - Mixed Martial Arts
Sports - Motorcycles and Motocross
Sports - Skateboarding
Sports - Skiing
Sports - Snowboarding
Sports - Soccer
Sports - Surfing and Boardsports
Sports - Tennis
Sports - Wrestling
Stand-up Comedy
Talk Shows
Thrillers
Westerns
Westerns - Action
Westerns - Comic
Westerns - Dramatic
Westerns - Musical
Westerns - Romantic

Index

Space for Your Own Notes

Make Money Online Using Zazzle

Amazon Video Direct is a wonderful passive income stream. Similar to writers, filmmakers complete their work one time and continue to earn revenue on the product for the rest of their life.

Those who love creativity might also check out this book on using Zazzle, a company that creates products on demand. If you can create graphic designs, take beautiful photography, paint a gorgeous picture, or write clever sayings, this might be an additional stream of income for you!

Imagine if you received an additional check each month...

Zazzle Tips from a Pro-Seller show you how to make money online using Zazzle, either as an Affiliate or as a designer. Learn to open an online store, establish a social media presence, and use tools such to save time and increase your Return on Investment (ROI).

- *Knowledge:* Learn what to know before opening a Zazzle business

- *Design Tricks:* Develop a plan for templates and Quick Create

- *Social Media Tips:* For Facebook, Twitter, Pinterest, YouTube, and Google+

- *Save Time:* Use auto-posting strategies for a better return on investment

- *Zazzle Affiliate Marketing:* Discover options for affiliate referral codes and RSS feeds

- *Rank Higher:* Learn SEO optimization tactics to help customers find you

- *Analytics:* Identify traffic sources and take action to increase visitors to make more money

Available for purchase at Amazon.com

Does your student have a Roth IRA yet?

From the Author: Recently I heard someone say they will not leave the world a better place (as is so often mentioned in the media today) but instead they will leave better children for the world.

Imagine if every child had a Roth IRA...

This book is to be used as a starting point for children and parents. The focus is on unmarried dependent children who begin working part time jobs through those that earn a full time salary.

Major Topics include:

1. *Money Management:* Appreciate the benefits of a Roth IRA

2. *Career Skills:* Identify different types of child employment

3. *New Ideas:* Discover different ways parents can employ their children

4. *Special Details:* Learn how parents can issue Forms W-2 for their child

5. *Introduction to Taxes:* Basic tax concepts for children with low earned income

6. *Powerful Knowledge:* Understand rules for children to contribute to a Roth IRA.

Available for purchase at <u>Amazon.com</u>

Prepare Early to Qualify for Federal Student Aid

Save thousands of dollars by starting early with a plan for college. Find explanations for: all the components that determine federal student aid, the better places to save, and what you should think about come tax time.

Imagine if every child had aid for college...

Major Topics include:

1. *Free Application for Federal Student Aid (FAFSA):* Quick overview

2. *Expected Family Contribution (EFC):* Detailed formula explanation

3. *Ideas for All Income Levels:* Take advantage of formula rules

4. *Tax-free and Tax-deferred Places to Save:* Explore investing options

5. *Education Accounts:* Choose the right one and who should own it

6. *Life Insurance:* Discover all the flexible uses

7. *Single or Divorced Parent:* Learn valuable strategies just for you

8. *College Offers:* Distinguish between free money and award of debt

9. *Tax Benefits for Education Expenses:* Make smart choices

Easily Order These Books

- at your local bookstore
- from the publisher at http://www.tracytrends.com
- online from Amazon.com

Review Request

If you would recommend this book to others, please consider writing a 5 star review on Amazon.com.

How to write a review in four easy steps:

1. On the Internet visit http://www.amazon.com
2. Enter 0-9814737-7-6 in the search box on Amazon
3. About half way down, click *Create Your Own Review*
4. Please tell others what you liked about this book

FREE Membership for Readers

Receive:
- Notification of book updates
- Amazon Video Direct news
- Video marketing strategies

View the link below to join:

https://www.KidsAndMoneyToday.com/avd/

Reader Comments and Inquiries

The best way to contact us is to sign up for our mailing list using the link above, and hit reply to any email you recieve. All comments, inquiries, or suggested updates will be condsidered for blog posts, newsletters, and future editions.

Find more tips for online marketing at:
https://www.KidsandMoneyToday.com
including links to connect with us on social networks:

www.ingramcontent.com/pod-product-compliance
Lightning Source LLC
Chambersburg PA
CBHW051248050326
40689CB00007B/1117